The Gallaudet
Children's
Dictionary
of American
Sign Language

a
b
c
d
e
f
g
h
i
j
k
l
m
n
o
p
q
r
s
t
u
v
w
x
y
z

The Gallaudet Children's Dictionary of American Sign Language

By the Editors of Gallaudet University Press

ASL CONSULTANT
Jean M. Gordon

COLOR ILLUSTRATIONS BY
Debbie Tilley

SIGN ILLUSTRATIONS BY
Peggy Swartzel Lott, Rob Hills, AND Daniel W. Renner

Gallaudet University Press   *Washington, DC*

a b c d e f g h i j k l m n o p q r s t u v w x y z

Gallaudet University Press

Washington, DC 20002

gupress.gallaudet.edu

10 9 8 7 6 5 4

Library of Congress Cataloging-in-Publication Data

The Gallaudet children's dictionary of American Sign Language / Jean M. Gordon, editorial consultant;

color illustrations by Debbie Tilley; sign illustrations by Peggy Swartzel Lott, Daniel Renner, and Rob Hills.

pages cm

Includes index.

ISBN 978-1-56368-631-3 (hardcover : alk. paper)—ISBN 1-56368-631-7 (hardcover)

1. American Sign Language—Dictionaries. 2. Deaf children—United States—Education.

I. Gordon, Jean. II. Tilley, Debbie, illustrator. III. Gallaudet University.

IV. Title: Children's dictionary of American Sign Language.

HV2475.G34995 2014

419'.703—dc23

2014004275

Printed in China

Cover and interior design by Joy Chu

Contents

a
b
c
d
e
f
g
h
i
j
k
l
m
n
o
p
q
r
s
t
u
v
w
x
y
z

Preface

The Gallaudet Children's Dictionary of American Sign Language is a dictionary for both deaf and hearing children. It serves a two-fold purpose—to teach American Sign Language (ASL), and to expand and improve English vocabulary skills.

It is designed primarily for children ages 5 and up—those just learning to read and independent readers. This dictionary will help children learn ASL and make connections between signs they already know and the written English words that express the same concepts. As a result, their reading vocabulary will grow, and they will gain an understanding of how English words can have different meanings. Parents, family members, and education professionals will also enjoy using this reference book.

The Gallaudet Children's Dictionary contains more than 1,000 ASL signs arranged in alphabetical order by the English word most commonly associated with each sign. This allows dictionary users to find specific signs more easily. The rest of the English words related to a given sign (synonyms) are listed under the main entry, and all the words appear in the index. In addition to the sign drawing, each entry includes a full-color illustration that is fun, whimsical, and instructive to reinforce the meaning of the sign/word, as well as a sentence using the word in context.

Speakers in different parts of a country use different words for the same concept. In the U.S., for example, people in the East say *soda*, while people in the Midwest say *pop*, and they both mean a carbonated beverage. Signers around the country also use different signs for the same concept. For instance, there are at least 17 signs for *Halloween* and 22 signs for *birthday*.[1] The differences often come from where a signer lives. Most of the signs in this dictionary are commonly used in everyday conversations at Gallaudet University and in the Washington, DC, area, which is a melting pot of ASL users from around the country.

The video content features children demonstrating the signs found in this dictionary. It also includes adults signing 150 sentences to demonstrate how to form sentences in ASL. The videos are available online at **gupress.gallaudet.edu.**

a
b
c
d
e
f
g
h
i
j
k
l
m
n
o
p
q
r
s
t
u
v
w
x
y
z

A C K N O W L E D G M E N T S

The editors thank Paul Kelly for his enthusiastic support throughout the development of this dictionary.

We also thank the following children and adults who modeled the signs for the book and the video:

Models for the Book	Child Models for the Video	Adult Models for the Video
Julia Burge	Julia Burge	Erin Oleson Dickson
Cameron Cruz	Cameron Cruz	Rudy Galicia
Dylan Ginther	Dylan Ginther	Blake Herbold
Reno Sophia Lott	Roxy Ginther	Pauline T. Saunders
Donavan Miller	Tayler Hamrick	
Patrick Miner-Smith	Reno Sophia Lott	
Lily Coral Molina	Donavan Miller	
Dakota Ronco	Winnie Miller	
Renny Savage	Lily Coral Molina	
Solomon Worthy	Dakota Ronco	
	Lenny Savage	
	Renny Savage	

Editorial and Production Staff

EDITORIAL DIRECTOR
Ivey Pittle Wallace

ASL CONSULTANT AND SIGN MASTER
Jean M. Gordon

COLOR ILLUSTRATIONS
Debbie Tilley

SIGN ILLUSTRATIONS AND VIDEO PRODUCTION
Peggy Swartzel Lott, Rob Hills, and Daniel W. Renner

EDITORIAL CONTRIBUTORS
Jill K. Porco
Lucie W. Brown
Marilyn Sass-Lehrer

EDITORIAL ASSISTANTS
Roberta Dunlap
Nelexis Garces
Katie Lee
Brenda Miers
Carla D. Morris
Anika Stephen

BOOK DESIGN AND PRODUCTION
Joy Chu

a
b
c
d
e
f
g
h
i
j
k
l
m
n
o
p
q
r
s
t
u
v
w
x
y
z

Introduction

American Sign Language (**ASL**) is the language used by members of the American Deaf community.[2] It is a language that developed from the interaction of signing deaf families, teachers, and students at the first deaf schools in the mid-18th to mid-19th centuries.

We don't know exactly how many people in the United States use ASL, but estimates range from 500,000 to 2 million.[3] This includes deaf children raised in deaf families; deaf children who learned to sign from hearing signing parents, teachers, and deaf classmates; hearing children born to deaf parents; and adults who learned ASL as a second language. ASL also is used widely in Canada, along with Quebec Sign Language. Every country in the world has its own sign language, and some countries (like Canada) have more than one sign language.

Some signs look like the object or idea they represent. For example, the sign for *tree* looks a lot like a tree, and the sign for *baby* looks like rocking a baby. These types of signs are called **iconic signs**. Other signs bear no resemblance to their meaning. The sign for *computer* does not look like a computer, and the sign for *store* does not look like a place to buy things. The fact that many signs are iconic does not mean that ASL is basically mime or a collection of "pictures in the air." It has its own vocabulary and grammar rules, just like other languages.

Most signers do not speak English while they sign, and the order of signs in an ASL sentence is often very different from

tree

baby

computer

store

the order of English words in a sentence. Signers also can convey grammatical information with their faces, bodies, and the surrounding space.

Fingerspelling

When signers want to emphasize the exact English word for a concept, they may spell the individual letters of the word. This is called **fingerspelling**. ASL has a specific handshape for each English letter, and all the handshapes are made on one hand. Every country has its own manual alphabet, and some countries, like England, form the letters with two hands. Signers also fingerspell when particular concepts, like personal names, geographical locations, and newly created words, do not have a sign. The easiest place to see fingerspelling is at mid-chest level. Signers hold their hand steady, and sometimes they mouth the word, but they don't say the individual letters.

ASL also has manual numbers, and almost all of them can be made on one hand. There are separate handshapes for numbers 1 to 15, 20, 21, 25, and 75. All other numbers are a combination of number handshapes. For example, 16 is a combination of 10 and 6; 38 is 3 and 8; 44 is 4 and 4; 50 is 5 and 0; and 1,256 is 1 + the sign for *thousand* + 2 + the sign for *hundred* + 5 + 6.

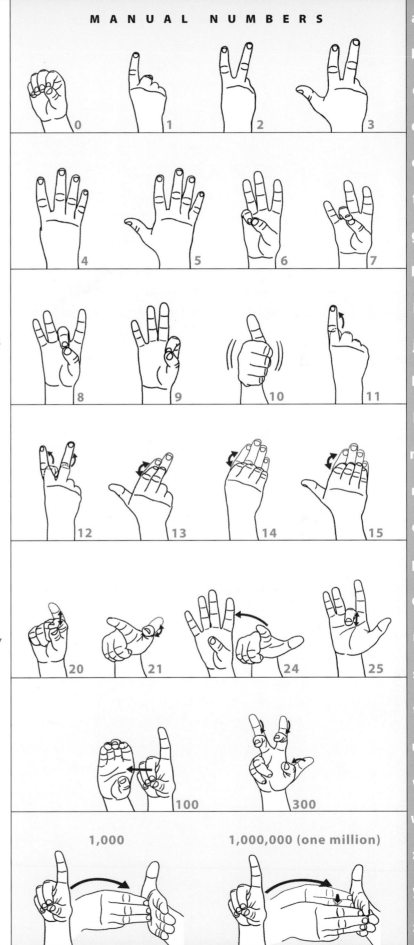

MANUAL NUMBERS

AMERICAN MANUAL ALPHABET

Aa

Bb

Cc

Dd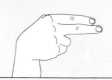

Ee

Ff

Gg

Hh

Ii

Jj

Kk

Ll

Mm

Nn

Oo

Pp

Qq

Rr

Ss

Tt

Uu

Vv

Ww

Xx

Yy

Zz

Signs

Signs are the vocabulary of ASL. Each sign represents a specific concept, and a sign cannot be used for an English word without considering its meaning. In English, the word *present* can mean "here" or "gift." ASL has a different sign for each meaning. Similarly, in English you can *run* a race, *run* for president, or *run* a company, and a signer will use a different sign in each case.

Each sign in ASL has five basic parts or parameters: *handshape, location, movement, palm orientation,* and *nonmanual signals.* Every sign includes all these parameters, so changing even one parameter creates a new sign. The signs *mother* and *father* share the same handshape, palm orientation, and movement, but they differ in location and, therefore, in meaning.

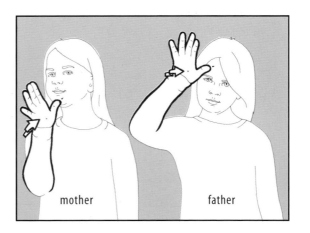

a
b
c
d
e
f
g
h
i
j
k
l
m
n
o
p
q
r
s
t
u
v
w
x
y
z

Handshape

Most of the handshapes used in ASL signs come from the American manual alphabet, from the manual numbers, and from modifications of those handshapes. Most of the time, the handshape is arbitrary or not important, but sometimes it carries a specific meaning. For example, the handshape for the sign *see* is a 2, but this handshape does not provide any additional meaning to the sign. However, when the 2 handshape is used with the signs for *hour, week, month,* and other time designations, it creates the meaning of 2 hours, 2 weeks, 2 months, and so forth.

Location

Location refers to the place where the hands start a sign. Almost all signs are made in the area between the forehead and the waist. The most comfortable position for signing, and the easiest place to see, is in front of the chest. At this level, people can see the hands and the face at the same time. This is important because signers use facial expressions to add information to their communication. A sign can begin on the body, on the head, or in the space in front of the body.

Movement

The way the hands move also is important to the meaning of signs. ASL does not add tense markers to signs to show future, present, and past. Instead, a signer will move the hand forward from the head to show that something will happen in the future, sign close to the body to show that something is happening now, or move the hand back over the shoulder to indicate that something has already happened.

A sign can move up, down, away from the signer, toward the signer, or side-to-side. There can be one single movement or multiple movements. Repeating the movement of a noun shows that the noun is plural rather than singular. For example, the sign *book* is made with one movement that resembles opening a book, while *books* repeats the movement. In *child,* the hand moves down slightly, but the hand bounces to the right a few times

past

present

future

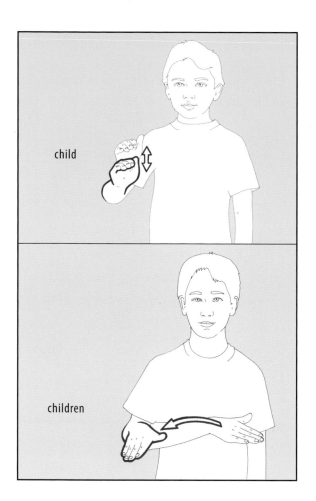

child

children

"I-look-at-you"

for "you-look-at-me" and "I-look-at-you" is in the orientation—facing in toward the signer and then out for "I-look-at-you" and facing out and then in toward the signer for "you-look-at-me."

Nonmanual Signals and Facial Expression

Facial expression is important in all forms of communication, but it is especially important in ASL. Deaf people focus on a signer's face as much as the hands. A signer can change the meaning of a word or phrase just by changing her expression. Most signs in everyday conversation are made with a neutral facial expression. However, there are signs that require a particular expression or nonmanual signal, like shrugging the shoulders or tilting the head forward, to make the meaning clear. The signs *who*, *what*, and *where* are good examples of how facial expressions and nonmanual signals are incorporated into a sign.

The illustrations in this dictionary include appropriate facial expressions, but to see the full effect of the nonmanual

for *children*, depending on the number of children.

With some verbs, the direction of the movement shows who is doing something, as in "I give it to you" (from the signer out to the other person) and "You give it to me" (from another person in to the signer). The size of the movement also contains meaning about volume or size. For example, it gets progressively larger to show the concepts *big, huge,* and *enormous*.

Orientation

The direction the palms face is called *orientation*. The palms can be up or down, toward the signer, or away from the signer. The difference between the signs

signals, watch the signs online. Beginning signers often forget about facial expressions; after all, it can be hard enough to remember where to put your hands. Just remember that your signing and ability to communicate will be enhanced by the use of facial expressions.

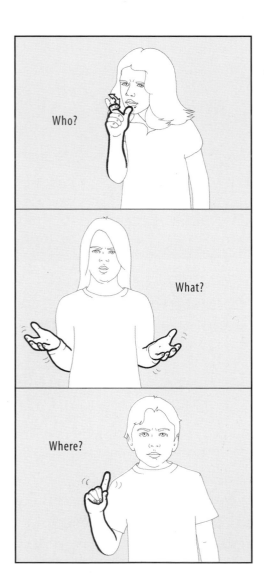

NOTES

1. Edgar H. Shroyer and Susan P. Shroyer collected regional signs for their book *Signs Across America* (Washington, DC: Gallaudet University Press, 1984).

2. In this dictionary, an uppercase D means the community of language users who are culturally Deaf. The members of the Deaf community share a language, values, and beliefs about deafness. A lowercase d refers to the deaf population in general and audiological deafness (the physiological condition of not being able to hear) in particular. Individuals who are deaf may not necessarily be Deaf.

3. Ross E. Mitchell, Travas A. Young, Bellamie Bachleda, Michael A. Karchmer, "How Many People Use ASL in the United States? Why Estimates Need Updating," *Sign Language Studies*, Volume 6, Number 3, Spring 2006, pp. 306–335.

How to Read This Dictionary

Some signs are made with one hand and others are made with two hands. Signers use their dominant hand to make one-hand signs. All of the models in this dictionary are right-handed, and the signs are drawn from the reader's perspective. Before copying a sign, right-handed signers should imagine themselves in the same position as the sign model. Left-handed signers should reverse the positions of the hands and the arrows and then mirror the signs on the page.

The beginning position of each sign is drawn with a thin line and the final position is drawn with a heavy line. Arrows indicate the direction of the sign movements.

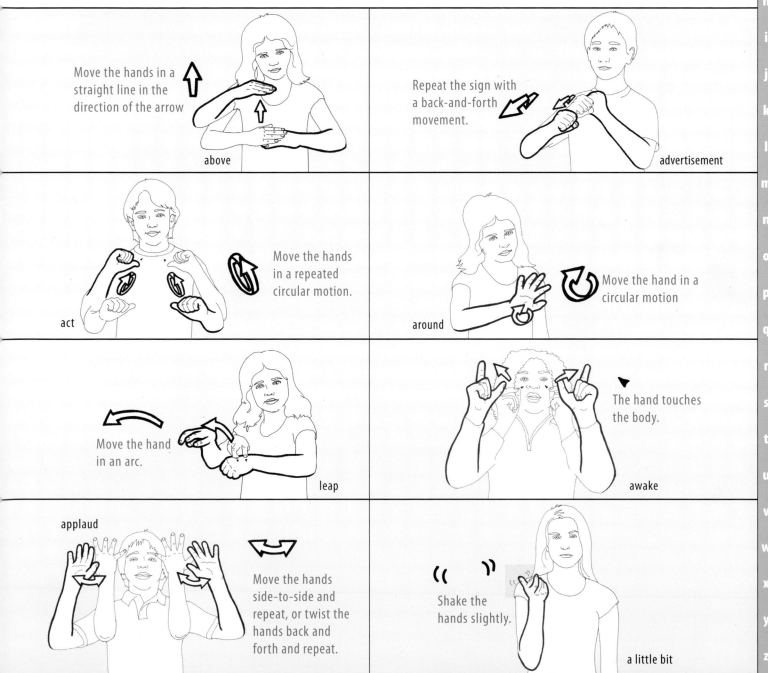

Move the hands in a straight line in the direction of the arrow

above

Repeat the sign with a back-and-forth movement.

advertisement

act

Move the hands in a repeated circular motion.

around

Move the hand in a circular motion

Move the hand in an arc.

leap

The hand touches the body.

awake

applaud

Move the hands side-to-side and repeat, or twist the hands back and forth and repeat.

Shake the hands slightly.

a little bit

Guide word: This is the first word on the left page.

Main English entries are in **red**.

Guide word: This is the last word on the right page.

New letter sections begin with the English capital and lowercase letters and the manual alphabet letter.

Arrows show how the hands move.

238 owl

owl
An **owl** hunts for food at night.

Pp

page
You read a book one **page** at a time.

pants 239

paint
How did I **paint** myself into a corner?

pancake
The top **pancake** gets the most syrup.

pants
jeans
slacks
trousers

Pants come in lots of shapes and colors.

Synonyms are listed below the main entry in **black**.

Highlighted letters mark the alphabet section.

ASL signs: The initial position is a thin, light line, and the final position is a heavy line.

Additional explanations in parentheses help clarify the meaning of the entry.

82 court

court
justice
trial

The judge controls the action in the **court**.

cousin (female)
Aunt Stacy and Uncle Jim's little girl is our **cousin**.

cousin (male)
Finally he met his Uncle Joe's son, his **cousin** who lives in India.

Sample sentences show how to use the main entry in an English sentence. The main word is in **red**.

A a

about

Grandpa tells many stories **about** his life.

above

over

A white bird flew **above** her head.

a b c d e f g h i j k l m n o p q r s t u v w x y z

accept

He was happy to **accept** the best teacher prize.

accident
car accident
collision

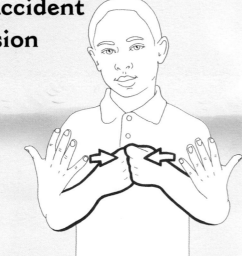

An **accident** happens when two cars hit each other.

accident
mistake

He did not knock over the paint on purpose; it was an **accident**.

across
cross over

Patty helps Granny go **across** the street.

act
perform

Tom loves to **act** on stage.

action
activity
deed
do

She likes the **action** of turning upside down.

a b c d e f g h i j k l m n o p q r s t u v w x y z

add
addition
additional
extra

Good cooks **add** just enough salt to the mix.

address
residence

The **address** tells where to send the letter.

adult

I will be the **adult** leader when I grow up.

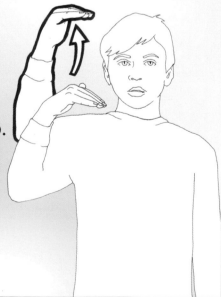

advertisement
ad

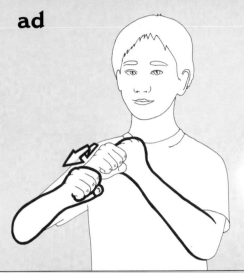

A good **advertisement** will attract many customers.

afraid
frightened
scared
terrified

This cat is **afraid** of a little mouse.

Africa

Africa is a very large continent.

a
b
c
d
e
f
g
h
i
j
k
l
m
n
o
p
q
r
s
t
u
v
w
x
y
z

after

Grandpa falls asleep **after** he lies down in the chair.

afternoon

Every day, she drinks tea at 2:00 in the **afternoon**.

again
over
repeat

The ride was so much fun, we did it again and **again**.

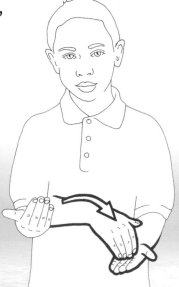

agree

They shook hands to **agree** on the price.

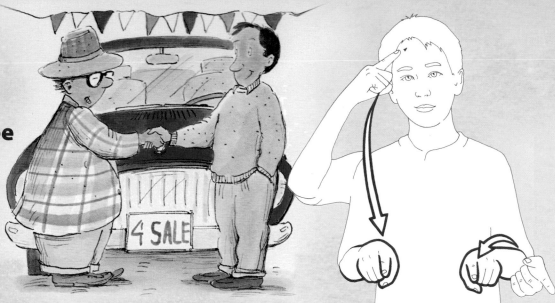

ahead

Turtle is so far **ahead** of Rabbit, he will win the race.

air conditioner

Spot likes to cool off in front of the **air conditioner**.

a b c d e f g h i j k l m n o p q r s t u v w x y z

a b c d e f g h i j k l m n o p q r s t u v w x y z

airplane

An **airplane** flies better in blue skies.

alarm

The **alarm** clock is loud to make people wake up.

a little bit

The fish need just **a little bit** of food, not a lot.

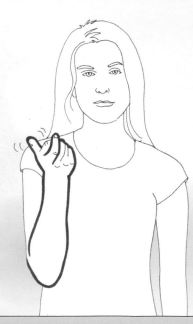

all
entire
total
whole

Sammy is tired from putting **all** the toys away.

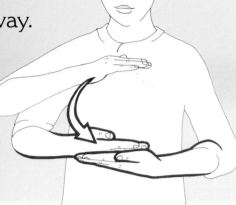

all day

Rain **all day** means no outside play.

all gone

The dog ate until his whole dinner was **all gone**.

a
b
c
d
e
f
g
h
i
j
k
l
m
n
o
p
q
r
s
t
u
v
w
x
y
z

a b c d e f g h i j k l m n o p q r s t u v w x y z

alligator

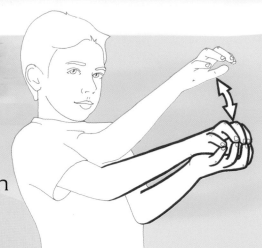

An **alligator** can live in the water or on land.

all night

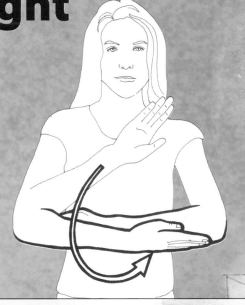

Spot howled **all night** at the moon.

allow

He will **allow** her to enter first.

all right

"Don't be sad. Everything will be **all right**."

almost
nearly

Emma can **almost**, but not quite, touch her shoes.

alone

Bobby wants to be **alone** without any friends in his treehouse.

a b c d e f g h i j k l m n o p q r s t u v w x y z

a b c d e f g h i j k l m n o p q r s t u v w x y z

a lot
much

Whales eat **a lot** of fish.

also
too

"I'll have ice cream on a brownie and **also** add a glass of milk."

always

Alex **always** hits the bullseye each time he shoots.

America

The Statue of Liberty is a symbol of **America**.

American Sign Language
ASL

1   **2**   **3**

Using **ASL** is a great way to say "I love you."

a
b
c
d
e
f
g
h
i
j
k
l
m
n
o
p
q
r
s
t
u
v
w
x
y
z

and

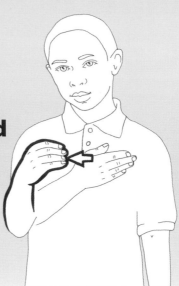

Tommy gave Santa a long list of toys **and** games.

angry

cross
furious
grouchy
grumpy
mad

Will is **angry** because he is in time out again.

animal

An **animal** lover has happy pets.

announce

The town crier rings the bell to **announce** the news.

answer

reply
report
respond
response

Percy always raises his hand to **answer** the question.

any

Pick a card, **any** card.

appear
pop up
show up

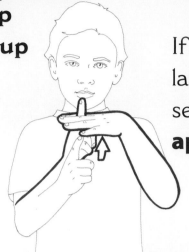

If you rub the lamp, you will see a genie **appear**.

appear
seem

How can a dog **appear** to float in the air?

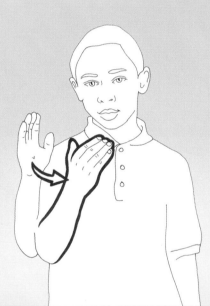

applaud (Deaf way)
applause

Deaf people **applaud** by waving their hands in the air.

apple

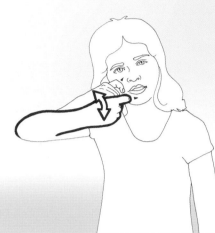

An **apple** is a tasty fruit.

arm

Jamie was surprised when the **arm** came off.

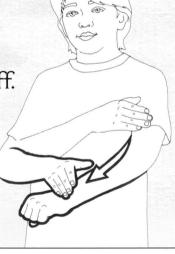

army
arms
military
soldier

My dad is a soldier in the **army**.

a
b
c
d
e
f
g
h
i
j
k
l
m
n
o
p
q
r
s
t
u
v
w
x
y
z

around
about
approximately

Babies start to walk when they are **around** 12 or 13 months old.

arrest

Police officers **arrest** robbers and put them in jail.

arrive

Who will **arrive** at the gate first—the man or the train?

artist

The **artist** likes to paint in the sunlight.

1

2

Asia

Asia is the largest continent.

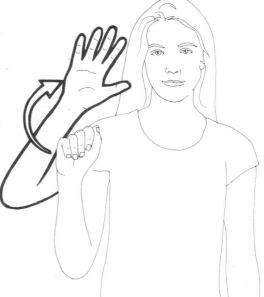

ask

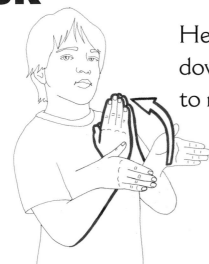

He kneeled down to **ask** her to marry him.

a b c d e f g h i j k l m n o p q r s t u v w x y z

attention
focus
pay attention

Sometimes he daydreams when he should pay **attention**!

audiologist

An **audiologist** tests hearing.

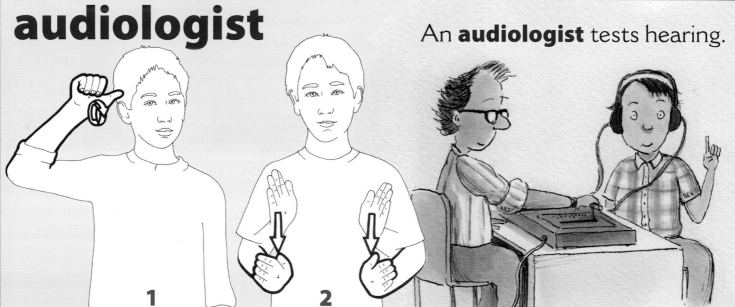

1   2

aunt

Aunt Jane is my mother's sister.

awake

Scary thoughts kept Juan **awake** all night.

awful

horrible
terrible

He knows the medicine will taste **awful**.

Now, You Know

Certain English words have a similar meaning, and the ASL signs for these words also are very similar. The only difference is the handshape. One example is the group of signs that mean *association, class, family, group, organization,* and *team* (see pages 69, 124, 153, and 314). The handshape for each sign is the first letter of the English word. Another group is the signs that mean *law, principle,* and *rule* (see pages 193 and 272).

a
b
c
d
e
f
g
h
i
j
k
l
m
n
o
p
q
r
s
t
u
v
w
x
y
z

a
b
c
d
e
f
g
h
i
j
k
l
m
n
o
p
q
r
s
t
u
v
w
x
y
z

Bb

baby

A **baby** will cry if he is hungry.

back

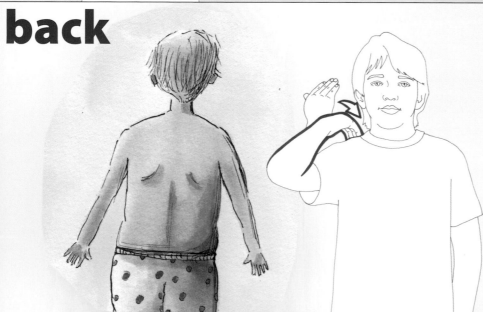

It is hard to scratch your own **back**.

back
return

The stray kitty came **back** every morning.

NOTE. **Back** can be signed toward the signer or away from the signer, depending on its meaning in the sentence.

backpack

Everything the boy needs is in his **backpack**.

bacon

Eggs go well with **bacon**.

a
b
c
d
e
f
g
h
i
j
k
l
m
n
o
p
q
r
s
t
u
v
w
x
y
z

a
b
c
d
e
f
g
h
i
j
k
l
m
n
o
p
q
r
s
t
u
v
w
x
y
z

bad
naughty

Sticking out your tongue is a **bad** thing to do.

bag

My cat loves to hide in a paper **bag**.

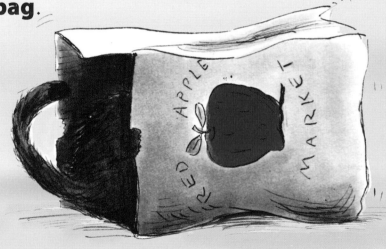

bake
oven

Bake the pie until the top is brown.

bald

Daddy's head is **bald** just like the baby's.

ball

He can spin a **ball** on one finger.

balloon

This **balloon** has a little bit too much air.

banana

A ripe **banana** is yellow.

bandage
Band-Aid

A **bandage** helps a finger to heal fast.

barber

The **barber** cut off all of Jordan's hair.

1   **2**

baseball

People love to play and watch **baseball**.

basement

The **basement** is below the first floor of the house.

basketball

Throw the **basketball** into the net to get points.

a
b
c
d
e
f
g
h
i
j
k
l
m
n
o
p
q
r
s
t
u
v
w
x
y
z

bat (animal)

The **bat** is the only mammal that can fly.

bath

You can wear a diving mask in a bubble **bath**.

bathroom
toilet

There is a toilet, a sink, and a tub in the **bathroom**.

beach

You can build sand castles at the **beach**.

bear

The brown **bear** hunted for fish.

beard

When I am old, I will grow a real **beard**.

a b c d e f g h i j k l m n o p q r s t u v w x y z

beautiful
lovely
pretty

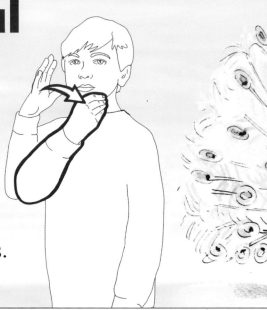

The bird spread its **beautiful**, colorful feathers.

bed

Late at night, a **bed** feels just right.

bee

A happy **bee** will not sting anyone.

before
prior to

Always look **before** you leap.

begin
commence
originate
start

The runners are ready to **begin** the race.

behave

"Act like a grown up and **behave** in the China Shop."

a b c d e f g h i j k l m n o p q r s t u v w x y z

behind
avoid
behind schedule

Lily was running **behind** schedule and missed the bus.

behind
in back of

The girl **behind** the tall people cannot see the show.

believe

From now on, Mary will **believe** fairies are real.

a
b
c
d
e
f
g
h
i
j
k
l
m
n
o
p
q
r
s
t
u
v
w
x
y
z

bell

When the **bell** rings, it makes a loud sound.

belong

attach
connect
join

The mitten and hat **belong** to Luke.

below

underneath

If the temperature drops **below** zero, carrots can't grow.

best

Spot won the prize for **best** dog in the show.

best friend

Anna plays with her **best friend** Liz every day.

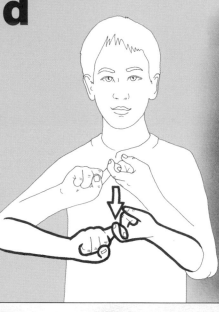

better

Granny can see much **better** with her new glasses.

bicycle
bike

You can ride a **bicycle** far and fast.

big
great
huge
large

The little baby looks up at the **big**, big man.

bird
chicken

The **bird** is washing its feathers.

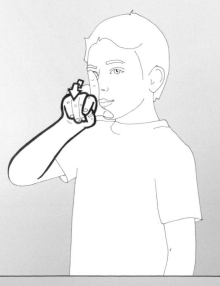

birthday

Your **birthday** happens once a year.

black

Black cats have yellow eyes.

blame

accuse

The boys **blame** each other for breaking the window.

blanket

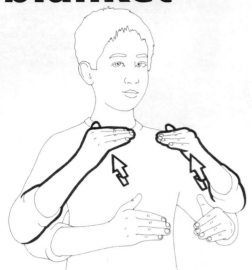

Hiding under a **blanket** can make you very hot.

blind

A **blind** mouse uses a cane to find his way.

NOTE. Many people now sign **blind** on the cheek below the right eye.

blood

Ice will make the **blood** stop dripping from his nose.

a
b
c
d
e
f
g
h
i
j
k
l
m
n
o
p
q
r
s
t
u
v
w
x
y
z

blouse

A **blouse** is a fancy kind of shirt.

blow

Blow too hard and the candles will fly off the cake.

blue
navy

He held his breath until he turned **blue**.

boat

A bathtub is a very unusual **boat**.

body

His **body** itches all over from poison oak.

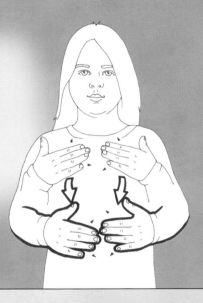

boil
burn

When the soup **boils**, bubbles form on top.

a
b
c
d
e
f
g
h
i
j
k
l
m
n
o
p
q
r
s
t
u
v
w
x
y
z

bologna
baloney
sausage

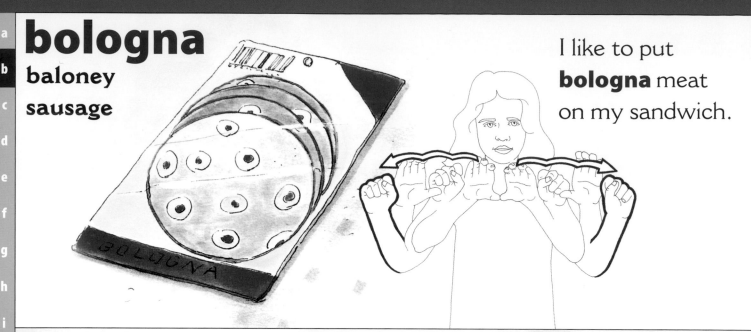

I like to put **bologna** meat on my sandwich.

bomb
explode

When this **bomb** stops ticking, it will go BOOM!

bones
skeleton

Archeologists search for old **bones**.

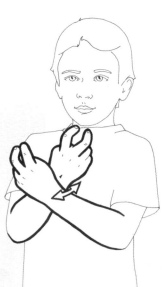

book
album
textbook

A **book** of fairy tales contains many stories.

bored
dull

Mike feels **bored** when he cannot ride his bike.

borrow

He wants to **borrow** a book from the library.

a
b
c
d
e
f
g
h
i
j
k
l
m
n
o
p
q
r
s
t
u
v
w
x
y
z

boss

capital
captain
chief

A **boss** tells you what to do at work.

bother

annoy
disturb
irritate

Ned is annoyed with flies that **bother** him.

bottle

The message in the **bottle** is far from the boat.

box   43

bowl

What color
is the mixing
bowl?

bowling

Bowling a strike is
the most fun!

box
package

Cats love to
play in a **box**.

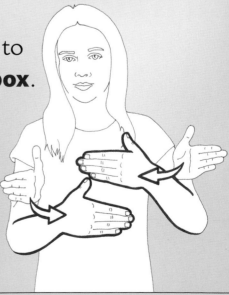

a
b
c
d
e
f
g
h
i
j
k
l
m
n
o
p
q
r
s
t
u
v
w
x
y
z

a
b
c
d
e
f
g
h
i
j
k
l
m
n
o
p
q
r
s
t
u
v
w
x
y
z

boy

This **boy** will grow to be a man.

brain

mind

You think of good ideas in your **brain**.

brave

courageous

The **brave** firefighter went in the burning building to save the child.

bread

Mary likes to feed **bread** to her ducks.

break
fracture

If you **break** a bone, friends will sign your cast.

break
midday break
take a break

He takes a nap during his **break** time.

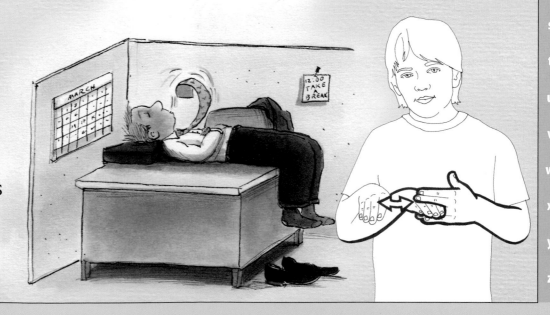

a
b
c
d
e
f
g
h
i
j
k
l
m
n
o
p
q
r
s
t
u
v
w
x
y
z

a
b
c
d
e
f
g
h
i
j
k
l
m
n
o
p
q
r
s
t
u
v
w
x
y
z

breakfast

NOTE. **Breakfast** can be signed two different ways.

Bill made plenty of pancakes for **breakfast**.

breathe

A snorkel helps you **breathe** under water.

bridge

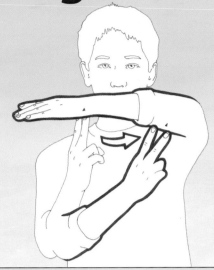

The **bridge** goes across the river.

brief
short

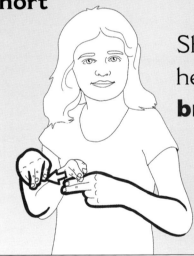

She could stay on her toes for only a **brief** time.

bring
brought
deliver

Some people say storks **bring** new babies to parents.

brother

My **brother** is the only boy in our family.

brown

Where is that other dark **brown** sock?

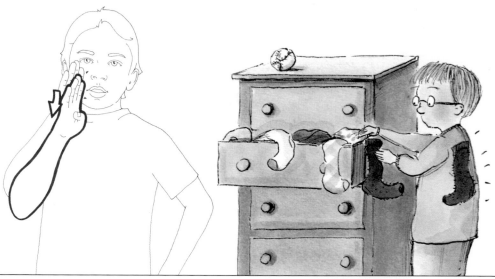

brush teeth

Hippos take a long time to **brush** their teeth.

buffalo

The American **buffalo** has a very hairy coat.

bug
insect

What kind of **bug** is this?

build
build up
construct

This dog likes to **build** dog houses.

a
b
c
d
e
f
g
h
i
j
k
l
m
n
o
p
q
r
s
t
u
v
w
x
y
z

a b c d e f g h i j k l m n o p q r s t u v w x y z

building

A skyscraper is a very tall **building**.

bull

An angry **bull** is dangerous.

bus

Many children ride a **bus** to school.

busy

The diner is a **busy** place on Saturday mornings.

but

although
different
however
unlike

He likes peas **but** not carrots.

butter

Do you put **butter** on your toast?

a b c d e f g h i j k l m n o p q r s t u v w x y z

butterfly

The beautiful **butterfly** has colorful wings.

button

A **button** popped off her coat.

buy
purchase

She went to the market to **buy** a fat pig.

Cc

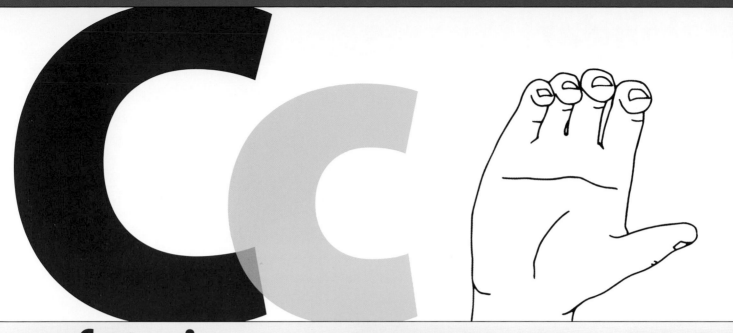

cafeteria

A **cafeteria** has many kinds of food.

cake

The birthday **cake** is covered with frosting.

a b c d e f g h i j k l m n o p q r s t u v w x y z

a
b
c
d
e
f
g
h
i
j
k
l
m
n
o
p
q
r
s
t
u
v
w
x
y
z

calendar
chart
schedule

We circled our vacation days on the **calendar**.

California

You can visit many places in the state of **California**.

call (on the phone)

The monkey ordered bananas with a phone **call**.

camera

Take a picture of your thumb with a **camera**.

can
could

Jump! You **can** do it!

Canada

The national flag of **Canada** is red and white.

a b c d e f g h i j k l m n o p q r s t u v w x y z

a
b
c
d
e
f
g
h
i
j
k
l
m
n
o
p
q
r
s
t
u
v
w
x
y
z

candle

A **candle** can light your way in the dark.

candy
cute

There are many delicious kinds of **candy**.

cannot
can't
couldn't
unable

Ask an adult for help when you **cannot** reach the shelf.

captions
closed captions
subtitles

If you cannot hear the TV, read the **captions**!

car
automobile
vehicle

Fixing a **car** can be dirty work.

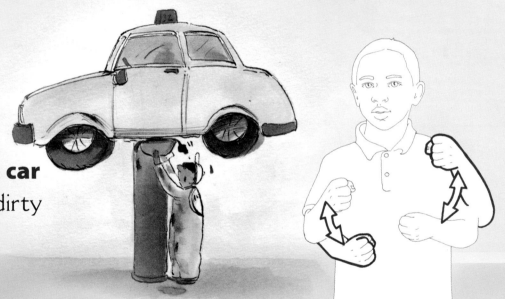

careful
keep
take care
watch out

Be **careful** and try not to spill the cups.

a b c d e f g h i j k l m n o p q r s t u v w x y z

a
b
c
d
e
f
g
h
i
j
k
l
m
n
o
p
q
r
s
t
u
v
w
x
y
z

careless
reckless

Rod is **careless** and sloppy when he gets dressed.

carpenter
woodworker

A beaver makes things out of wood, just like a **carpenter**.

carrot

People usually eat the orange part of a **carrot**.

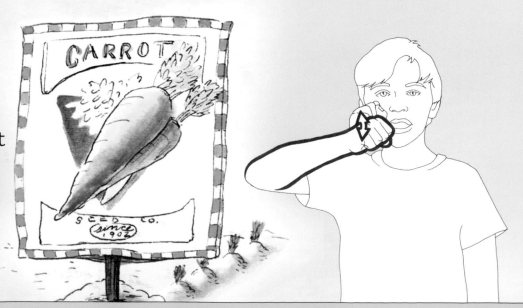

carry

Max can **carry** a lot of popcorn!

cat

The fat **cat** purrs at dinnertime.

catch

apprehend

nab

Spot helps the police **catch** robbers.

a
b
c
d
e
f
g
h
i
j
k
l
m
n
o
p
q
r
s
t
u
v
w
x
y
z

catch
catch a ball

Jenny can **catch** the ball in her glove.

caterpillar

A **caterpillar** becomes a moth or butterfly.

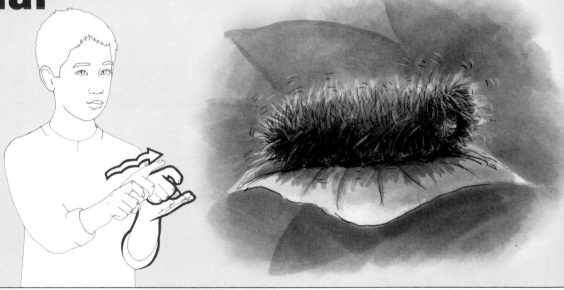

Catholic

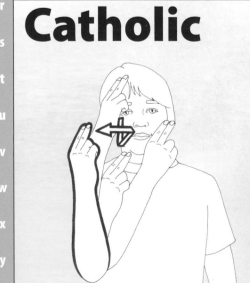

The Pope is the head of the **Catholic** Church.

ceiling

Painting a **ceiling** is hard work.

celebrate

anniversary
celebration
festival
holiday
victory

The cheerleaders **celebrate** when their team wins!

center

central
middle

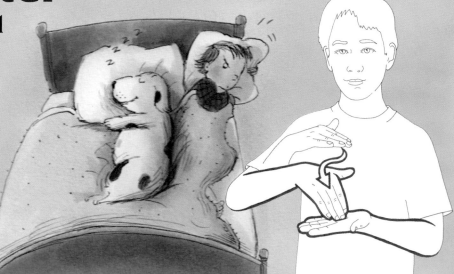

Spot likes to sleep in the **center** of the bed.

a b c d e f g h i j k l m n o p q r s t u v w x y z

a
b
c
d
e
f
g
h
i
j
k
l
m
n
o
p
q
r
s
t
u
v
w
x
y
z

cereal

Do you eat **cereal** for breakfast?

chain

NO DOGS ALLOWED

The **chain** keeps the dog tied up outside.

chair
seat

A soft **chair** is a comfortable place to sit.

chalk

Ella draws pretty pictures with colored sidewalk **chalk**.

change

adapt
adjust
alter
modify

Chameleons **change** color to match almost anything.

chapter

Chapter 3 of the book was really sad.

a
b
c
d
e
f
g
h
i
j
k
l
m
n
o
p
q
r
s
t
u
v
w
x
y
z

a b c d e f g h i j k l m n o p q r s t u v w x y z

chase

Molly likes to **chase** butterflies with her net.

cheat

You should not **cheat** by looking at your friend's answers.

checkers

The game of **checkers** was invented 400 hundred years ago.

cheese

This mouse wants to eat that **cheese**.

cherry

Most desserts taste better with a **cherry** on top.

child

Little Tommy is a happy **child**.

a b c d e f g h i j k l m n o p q r s t u v w x y z

a b c d e f g h i j k l m n o p q r s t u v w x y z

children

Children enjoy story time with the teacher.

China

China is an ancient and beautiful country.

chocolate
cocoa

Chocolate is the most popular ice cream flavor.

choose
pick
select

Dylan hopes to **choose** the right cup.

Christmas

Who put the **Christmas** presents under the tree?

church
chapel

People go to **church** to pray.

a b c d e f g h i j k l m n o p q r s t u v w x y z

a
b
c
d
e
f
g
h
i
j
k
l
m
n
o
p
q
r
s
t
u
v
w
x
y
z

circle
orbit
round

Sharks **circle** around when they are hungry.

NOTE. The orientation of the hand reflects the location of the object.

circus
clown

You will see acrobats and animals at the **circus**.

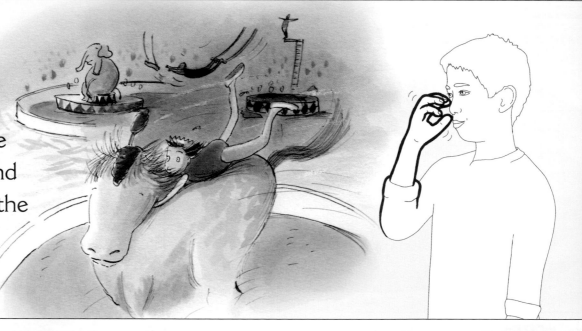

city
downtown
uptown

A big **city** has many tall buildings.

clap

applaud (hearing way)
praise

People **clap** their hands when they like something.

class

The music **class** students play their instruments with joy.

clean

neat
nice
pure
tidy

Terry's **clean** clothes will dry on the line.

a b c d e f g h i j k l m n o p q r s t u v w x y z

a
b
c
d
e
f
g
h
i
j
k
l
m
n
o
p
q
r
s
t
u
v
w
x
y
z

clean up

After the movie, Kevin has to **clean up** the theater.

clear
bright
light

Jose can see fish and plants in the **clear** water.

climb

Shane had to **climb** up the tree to pick the apples.

clock

Look at the **clock** to see the time.

close
shut

At 5:00 the store will **close**.

close the door

The closet is so full, he can't **close the door**.

close the window
shut the window

Did a strong breeze **close the window** on her long hair?

clothes
apparel
garment

Alex doesn't like to try on new **clothes**.

coat
jacket
overcoat

Ruby does not need a **coat** to stay warm.

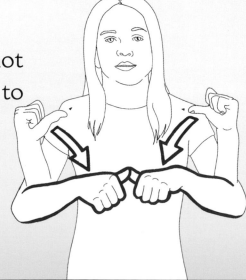

a
b
c
d
e
f
g
h
i
j
k
l
m
n
o
p
q
r
s
t
u
v
w
x
y
z

coffee

Grown-ups like to drink **coffee** in a cup.

Coke
Coca-Cola

Coke is one type of soda pop.

NOTE. Some people fingerspell **Coke**.

cold (illness)
head cold

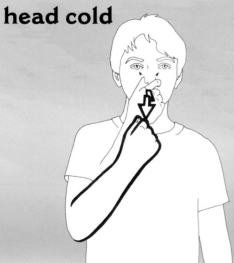  

Spot is sneezing because he has a **cold**.

cold (temperature)
chilly
frigid
winter

People from the north like **cold** weather.

collapse
breakdown

Adding the last ace made the cards **collapse**.

color

Her hair turned a bright green **color**.

comb

Pete uses a **comb** to fix his hair.

come

I hope you can **come** to my party.

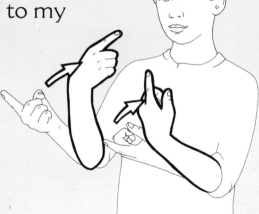

come here

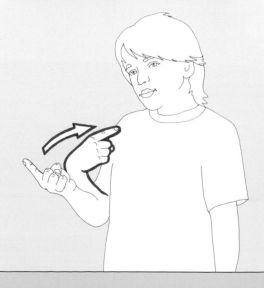

Mom said, "**Come here**, Spot; it's time for your bath."

a b c d e f g h i j k l m n o p q r s t u v w x y z

a
b
c
d
e
f
g
h
i
j
k
l
m
n
o
p
q
r
s
t
u
v
w
x
y
z

come on

Come on and ride the bike with me!

comfortable

comfort

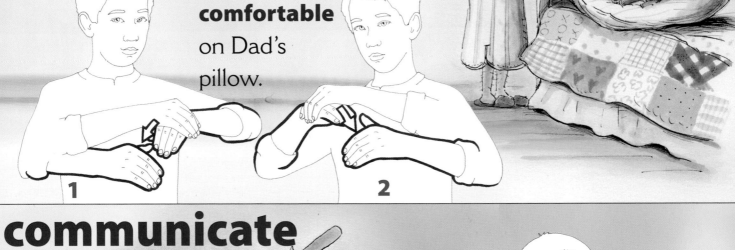

The cat is cozy and **comfortable** on Dad's pillow.

1

2

communicate

communication
conversation

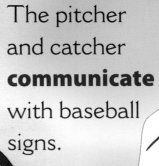

The pitcher and catcher **communicate** with baseball signs.

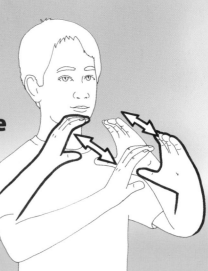

compare
comparison

He will **compare** two very different fruits.

computer

You can write and save your work on a **computer**.

confused
mixed up

The mixed-up directions on the sign **confused** the man.

a
b
c
d
e
f
g
h
i
j
k
l
m
n
o
p
q
r
s
t
u
v
w
x
y
z

a
b
c
d
e
f
g
h
i
j
k
l
m
n
o
p
q
r
s
t
u
v
w
x
y
z

congratulations
congratulate

Grandpa said,
"**Congratulations**
on your new baby!"

continue

endure
last
permanent
persevere

He will **continue**
climbing all the
way to the top.

control

direct
govern
manage
rule
run

Sam can **control** the robot's actions.

cook
cooking
fry

She likes to **cook** pots full of good food.

cookie

Who will eat the last **cookie**?

cooperate
cooperation

The sisters will **cooperate** to reach the cookie jar.

corn

Corn on the cob tastes great!

correct
right

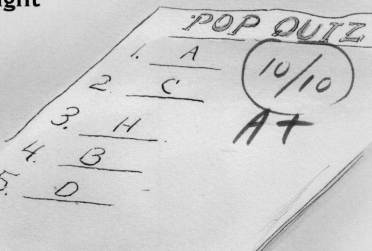

All of the answers are **correct**.

cost
charge
fare
fee
fine
price
tax

The **cost** of gum has gone up a lot.

cough

Cover your mouth if you have to **cough**.

count

22, 23, 24...

Emma likes to **count** her Halloween candy.

country
foreign

You need a passport to travel to a different **country**.

a b c d e f g h i j k l m n o p q r s t u v w x y z

a
b
c
d
e
f
g
h
i
j
k
l
m
n
o
p
q
r
s
t
u
v
w
x
y
z

court
justice
trial

The judge controls the action in the **court**.

cousin (female)

Aunt Stacy and Uncle Jim's little girl is our **cousin**.

cousin (male)

Finally he met his Uncle Joe's son, his **cousin** who lives in India.

COW
cattle

A **cow** eats grass and then makes milk.

cracker
Passover

A good **cracker** is crisp and salty.

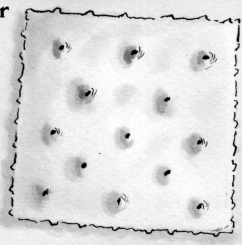

crash

Kitty made the glass **crash** to the ground.

NOTE. The movement of the hand reflects the direction of the crash.

a b c d e f g h i j k l m n o p q r s t u v w x y z

a b c d e f g h i j k l m n o p q r s t u v w x y z

crawl
baby crawling

Babies **crawl** before they can walk.

cry
weep

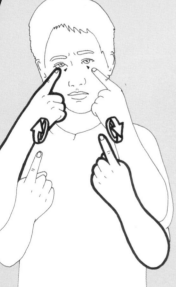

If you **cry** hard, maybe you can fill a bucket.

culture

Playing the bagpipes is an old tradition in Scottish **culture**.

cup

can

glass

jar

A **cup** with a lid helps prevent spills.

curious

The boy is **curious** about what is in the box.

curtains

drapes

Open **curtains** let the light in.

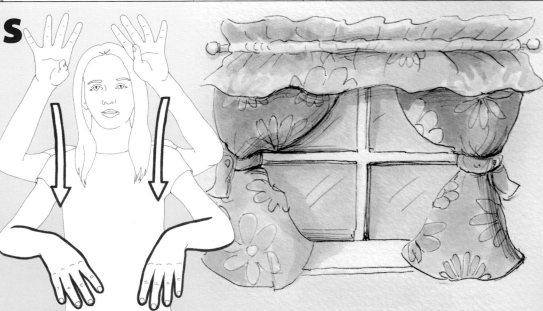

a b c d e f g h i j k l m n o p q r s t u v w x y z

cut
scratch

Dad **cut** his finger on a piece of paper.

NOTE. **Cut** is signed on the body part where the cut occurs.

cut (paper)

Lucy loves to **cut** out pink paper dolls.

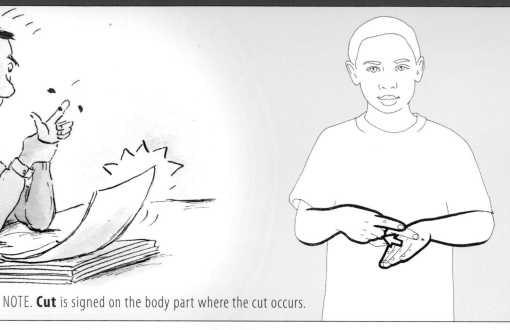

cute

She thinks his cheeks are **cute**.

Dd

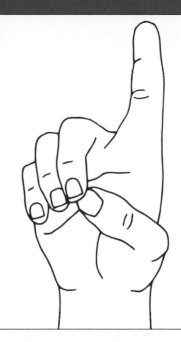

daily
every day
everyday

The **daily** newspaper arrives early every morning.

dance

All dogs **dance** at the Bow-Wow Ball.

a
b
c
d
e
f
g
h
i
j
k
l
m
n
o
p
q
r
s
t
u
v
w
x
y
z

danger
dangerous
risk
unsafe

Slipping on a banana peel can be a **danger** to your bones!

dark

He keeps a nightlight on to see in the **dark**.

day

This year on Mother's **Day**, she got flowers.

dead
death
die

Opossums play **dead** if they sense danger.

deaf

Deaf people can sign with friends and family on videophones.

decide
decision

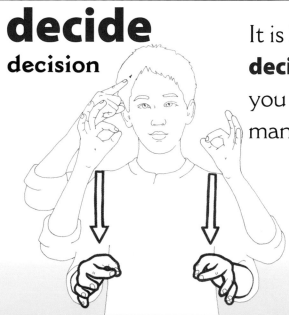

It is hard to **decide** when you have many choices.

eeny meeny....

a
b
c
d
e
f
g
h
i
j
k
l
m
n
o
p
q
r
s
t
u
v
w
x
y
z

decorate

Betty likes to **decorate** for a party.

deep
depth

Billy saw a lot of strange fish in the **deep** blue sea.

deer

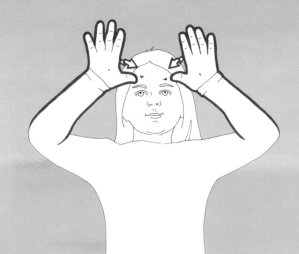

Female **deer** don't have antlers.

a b c d e f g h i j k l m n o p q r s t u v w x y z

delete
eliminate

If Baby presses the **delete** key, Mommy's typing will be gone!

delicious
tasty

The banana split sundae was **delicious**!

dentist

The **dentist** is brushing a giant's tooth.

a b c d e f g h i j k l m n o p q r s t u v w x y z

a b c d e f g h i j k l m n o p q r s t u v w x y z

dependable
count on
depend on
rely on

Our **dependable** mail carrier brings our letters every day.

desk
table

She stands on a chair to work at this **desk**.

dessert

How many pieces of **dessert** can you eat?

detective

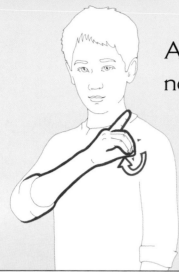

A good **detective** notices everything.

devil

**demon
evil
mischief
wicked**

Many people believe a **devil** does bad things.

dice

gamble

Roll a seven with the **dice** and you win!

a b c d e f g h i j k l m n o p q r s t u v w x y z

dictionary

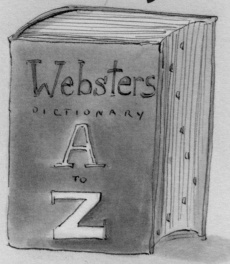

You can find the meaning of "flapdoodle" in the **dictionary**.

difficult

hard
problem

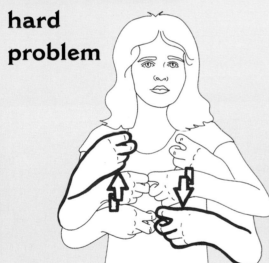

This exercise is **difficult** without a stool.

dime

ten cents

A **dime** is worth ten cents, and ten dimes make a dollar.

dinner

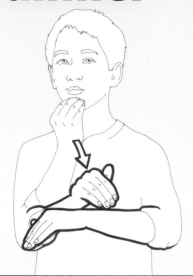

He roasted a hot dog for his **dinner**.

NOTE. **Dinner** can be signed two ways.

dinosaur

Billy dressed as a tiny **dinosaur** on Halloween.

a b c d e f g h i j k l m n o p q r s t u v w x y z

a
b
c
d
e
f
g
h
i
j
k
l
m
n
o
p
q
r
s
t
u
v
w
x
y
z

dirt
earth
ground
land
sand
soil

Spot can dig up plenty of **dirt**!

dirty
filthy

messy

Getting **dirty** is fun until you have to wash.

disagree

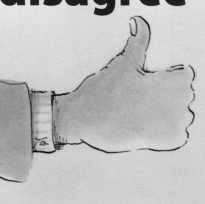

We **disagree** on which movie is better.

disappear
vanish

The magic potion made his homework **disappear**.

discuss
debate
discussion

The explorers **discuss** the plans for their trip.

disgusting
gross

Your feet smell **disgusting**!

a
b
c
d
e
f
g
h
i
j
k
l
m
n
o
p
q
r
s
t
u
v
w
x
y
z

dissolve

cure
fade
melt
solution
solve

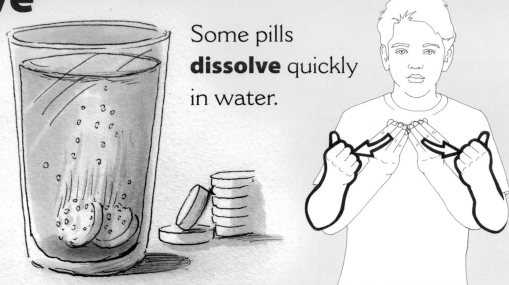

Some pills **dissolve** quickly in water.

dive

Dive into the ocean with a neat splash!

divide

split

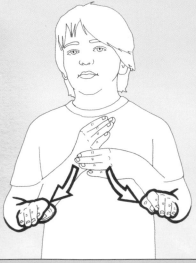

You can **divide** the cheese in half to get two equal parts.

divorce

Some people **divorce** if they have an unhappy marriage.

do
act
behave

Blocks can't move or **do** anything themselves.

doctor
physician

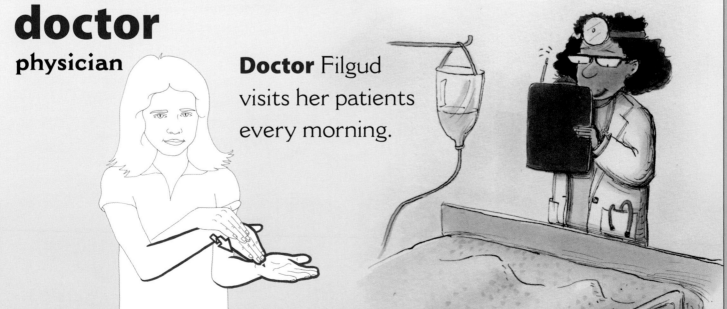

Doctor Filgud visits her patients every morning.

a b c d e f g h i j k l m n o p q r s t u v w x y z

a
b
c
d
e
f
g
h
i
j
k
l
m
n
o
p
q
r
s
t
u
v
w
x
y
z

dog

Our **dog** Spot always barks at red fire plugs.

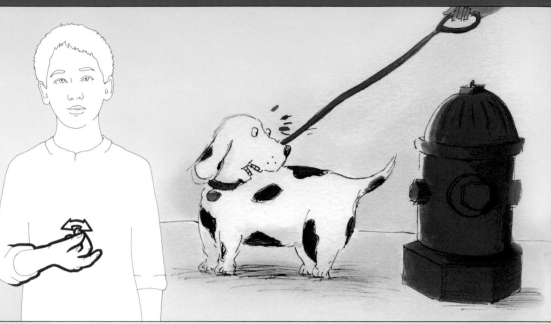

doll
toy

She loves her rag **doll.**

dollar

George Washington's picture is on a one **dollar** bill.

donkey

A **donkey** is a useful work animal.

don't

Don't blow bubbles while I am painting!

don't care

"Do you want to play in the front or backyard?"

"I **don't care**, you pick."

a b c **d** e f g h i j k l m n o p q r s t u v w x y z

don't know
unknown
unsure

I **don't know** the answer to the question.

don't like
dislike
does not like

If you **don't like** it, don't spill it!

don't want

I **don't want** you to follow me!

door

The bookcase opens like a **door** to a secret room.

dormitory
dorm

A **dormitory** is a place where students live.

doughnut

Have a **doughnut** with sprinkles for dessert.

a b c d e f g h i j k l m n o p q r s t u v w x y z

down

Skiing feels like flying **down** a mountain.

NOTE. **Down** can be signed straight down or at an angle.

draw
illustrate

She likes to **draw** what she sees outside.

drawing
illustration

Self Portrait

JUDY B.
AGE 5

She entered her **drawing** in the art show.

dream
fantasy

Spot had a **dream** about being a super dog.

dress
apparel
clothes
fashion
garment

She looks pretty in her new Christmas **dress**.

dress
get dressed

It is easy to **dress** when you have all your clothes.

a
b
c
d
e
f
g
h
i
j
k
l
m
n
o
p
q
r
s
t
u
v
w
x
y
z

drink
beverage

The curly straw
makes the **drink**
last longer.

drive

Billy will **drive** as fast as he can walk.

drop
dump

Football players try not
to **drop** the ball.

drums

Pots and pans make excellent **drums**.

dry
arid

Soon, these clothes will be **dry** and warm.

duck

A **duck** can swim and fly.

a
b
c
d
e
f
g
h
i
j
k
l
m
n
o
p
q
r
s
t
u
v
w
x
y
z

a b c d e f g h i j k l m n o p q r s t u v w x y z

due
**debt
owe**

Her books are **due** back in the library today.

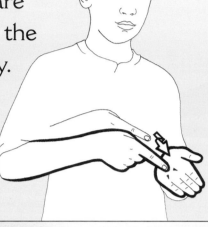

dumb
**ignorant
stupid**

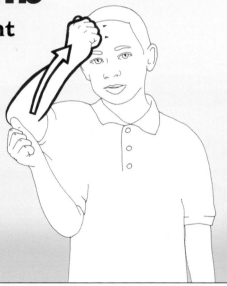

Spot felt **dumb** after his head got stuck in the jar.

Now, You Know

Deaf people have different ways to get each other's attention. Since they can't call to each other from another room, they go to the room and flash the light near the door. This lets the other person know that someone is there. Deaf people also put light flashers on their doorbells, videophones, baby monitors, alarm clocks, and other devices.

Ee

each

apiece
every

Each snowflake has a different shape.

each other

associate
interact
mutual

The boys like to play checkers against **each other**.

a b c d **e** f g h i j k l m n o p q r s t u v w x y z

a b c d **e** f g h i j k l m n o p q r s t u v w x y z

eagle

The **eagle** is proud and fierce.

ear

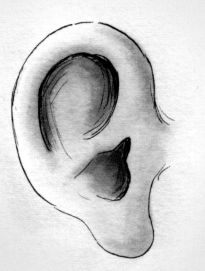

We can see only the outer part of the **ear**.

ear ache

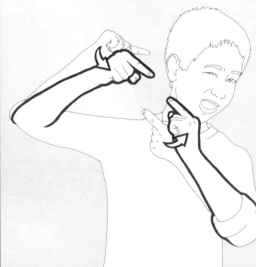

An **ear ache** is very painful.

early

You have to get up **early** to catch a fish.

Earth
geography

We all need to take care of the **Earth**.

east

The ship will sail **east** toward the sunrise.

Easter

The **Easter** bunny left an egg on our lawn.

easy

These problems are **easy** if you know how to add.

eat
dine

The winner has to **eat** a lot of pie!

egg

Open an **egg** and cook it for breakfast.

elbow

Keep your **elbow** inside your seat!

electric

**battery
electricity**

An **electric** guitar can make lots of noise!

a b c d e f g h i j k l m n o p q r s t u v w x y z

a b c d e f g h i j k l m n o p q r s t u v w x y z

elephant

The **elephant** can do tricks with its trunk.

elevator

She takes the **elevator** to the fifth floor.

e-mail

E-mail is an excellent way to send a message.

empty
available
bare
blank
space
vacant

When school is closed, the classroom is **empty**.

encyclopedia

Ellen learns about everything in the **encyclopedia**.

end
complete
last

The girls cried at the **end** of the movie.

a
b
c
d
e
f
g
h
i
j
k
l
m
n
o
p
q
r
s
t
u
v
w
x
y
z

enemy
foe
opponent
rival

The gardener fights with her **enemy** the gopher.

English
England

The **English** royal guards protect the queen.

enjoy
appreciate
enjoyable
enjoyment
like
take pleasure in

She likes to relax and **enjoy** the water on Sundays.

enough
adequate
sufficient

That's **enough** coffee, but I need more sugar.

enter
entrance
go into
into

Stay alert when you **enter** an underwater cave.

envelope
blank check

She sealed each **envelope** carefully.

a b c d e f g h i j k l m n o p q r s t u v w x y z

a b c d **e** f g h i j k l m n o p q r s t u v w x y z

equal
even
fair
just
tie

Mom is fair and gives them **equal** amounts of dessert.

erase (a board)

If you **erase** the white board, it will be blank.

erase (on paper)

Use a pencil so you can **erase** your mistakes.

escape

flee

get away

run away

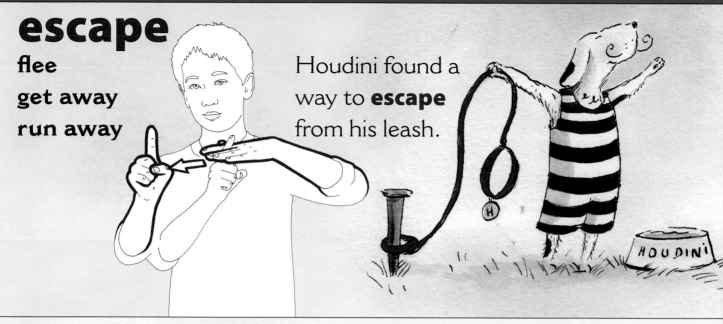

Houdini found a way to **escape** from his leash.

Europe

The continent of **Europe** has many countries.

event

excite

thrill

what's up?

The sack race is our favorite field day **event**!

a
b
c
d
e
f
g
h
i
j
k
l
m
n
o
p
q
r
s
t
u
v
w
x
y
z

everything

The phone is buried under **everything** on his desk.

excited

excitement
exciting

The team was really **excited** about winning the trophy.

excuse me

Excuse me—my shoelace is under your foot.

exercise

Exercise will keep you fit and healthy.

explain
explanation

Aubrey must **explain** why she doesn't have her homework.

eyes

Some women cover all of themselves except their **eyes**.

a
b
c
d
e
f
g
h
i
j
k
l
m
n
o
p
q
r
s
t
u
v
w
x
y
z

a b c d e f g h i j k l m n o p q r s t u v w x y z

Ff

face

appearance

A pie in the **face** might not taste very good.

fail

You **fail** the test if your answers are wrong.

fall
autumn

Fall leaves are beautiful, but we must rake them.

fall

Beginning ice skaters **fall** a lot.

false
artificial
counterfeit
fake
imposter
pseudo
untrue

If the answer is wrong, check **false**.

True

False

family

I love everyone in my **family**, especially Willy.

famous

Davy Crockett is well known as a **famous** folk hero.

far
distant

Last night, Max saw stars **far** from Earth.

farm

Farmer Svensen grows wheat on his **farm**.

fast
immediate
quick
rapid
speedy
swift

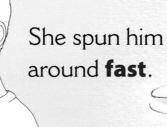

She spun him around **fast**.

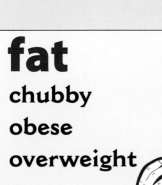

fat
chubby
obese
overweight

This cat is **fat** and happy!

a
b
c
d
e
f
g
h
i
j
k
l
m
n
o
p
q
r
s
t
u
v
w
x
y
z

father
dad
daddy

The **father** always lets his son catch the big fish.

fault

She bumped into him, so it is her **fault** he dropped the glass.

favorite
prefer
preference
want

Bobby takes his **favorite** monkey everywhere.

feed

Otis makes a mess when his Grandma **feeds** him.

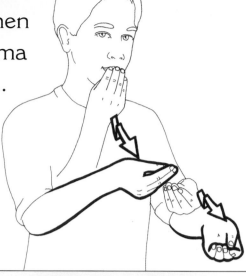

feel

feelings
felt
sensation
sense

I **feel** like someone is watching me.

feet

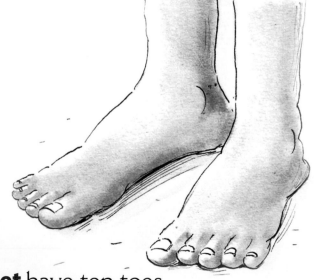

Most **feet** have ten toes.

fence

The cat is tiptoeing across the **fence**.

few
several

The pumpkin has just a **few** teeth.

fight
fighting

Most cats enjoy a good pillow **fight**.

a
b
c
d
e
f
g
h
i
j
k
l
m
n
o
p
q
r
s
t
u
v
w
x
y
z

find
discover
well

Spot had to dig
five holes to
find his bone.

fine
okay
well

I am **fine**, but
my bike is not!

finger

The ring is stuck on
his **finger**.

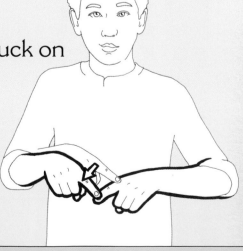

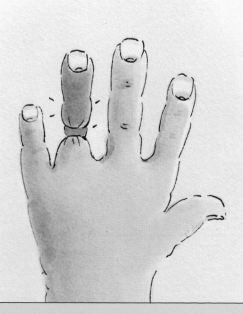

a b c d e f g h i j k l m n o p q r s t u v w x y z

fingers

He plays so fast that ten **fingers** look like dozens!

fingerspelling
spelling

Her **fingerspelling** is very clear.

finish
already
complete
did
done
over
through

Jon was happy to **finish** the race.

fire
flames

A small **fire** will keep you warm on a cold night.

firefighter

The **firefighter** put out the flames to save the building.

first
original

George Washington was our **first** president.

a b c d e f g h i j k l m n o p q r s t u v w x y z

a
b
c
d
e
f
g
h
i
j
k
l
m
n
o
p
q
r
s
t
u
v
w
x
y
z

fish

Mr. Brown likes his big pet **fish**.

fishing

He is **fishing** for trout for tonight's dinner.

fix

Turn off the water before you **fix** the faucet.

flag

On national holidays, we proudly wave our **flag**.

flat

A long time ago, people believed the Earth was **flat**.

flat tire

When the car ran over sharp rocks, it got a **flat tire**.

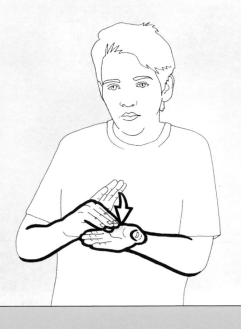

floor

A loose board in the **floor** can be squeaky.

flower

Bea took a nap on the **flower**.

fly
bird flying

Do you believe that pigs can **fly**?

a b c d e f g h i j k l m n o p q r s t u v w x y z

follow

go after
pursue
track

Spot will **follow** the smell of yummy food until he finds it.

food

groceries
meal

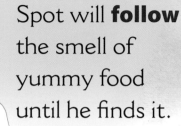

Eating the right **food** keeps you healthy.

football

Kick, pass, and catch a **football** for fun.

for

Jake was a pirate **for** Halloween.

forbid
ban
illegal
prohibit

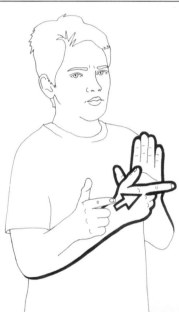

I **forbid** you to go across the busy street.

forest
jungle
woods

Hansel and Gretel got lost in the pine tree **forest**.

forget
because

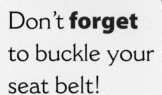

Don't **forget** to buckle your seat belt!

fork

A **fork** has pointed tines to pick up food.

fox

The **fox** stood quietly in the snow.

a b c d e f g h i j k l m n o p q r s t u v w x y z

a
b
c
d
e
f
g
h
i
j
k
l
m
n
o
p
q
r
s
t
u
v
w
x
y
z

France
French

Visitors love the food in the country of **France**.

free
freedom
liberty

She did not have to pay for the **free** sample.

TAKE ONE

freeze
freezer
frozen
ice

When you **freeze** water, it becomes ice.

French fries

French fries are a delicious treat.

Friday

Friday is the best day of the week!

friend
friendship

Tom and his **friend** Huck do lots of things together.

a
b
c
d
e
f
g
h
i
j
k
l
m
n
o
p
q
r
s
t
u
v
w
x
y
z

frog

The **frog** sits on a lily pad floating in a pond.

front

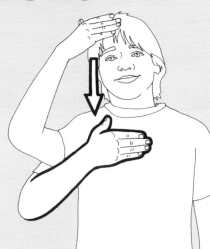

Charlie sat in **front** with the driver.

fruit

Dolores has lots of **fruit** on her hat.

full
complete
filled

Evan's suitcase is too **full** to close.

full (of food)
sated
satisfied

Spot feels **full** from eating so many dog biscuits.

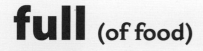

fun
leisure
recreation

Sledding down a snowy hill is great winter **fun**.

a b c d e f g h i j k l m n o p q r s t u v w x y z

funny
amusing
humorous

Joe does **funny** things to make me laugh.

furniture

His parents are shopping for new **furniture**.

future
someday
will

Madam Moonlight can see what will happen in the **future**.

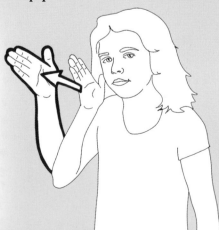

Gg

game

Hide and seek is a fun **game**.

garage

The car fits perfectly in the **garage**.

a b c d e f g h i j k l m n o p q r s t u v w x y z

garbage
refuse

trash

waste

Garbage can smell really bad!

gas
gasoline

Cars need **gas** to run.

Germany
German

Fall festivals in **Germany** include good food and music.

get

acquire

catch

obtain

receive

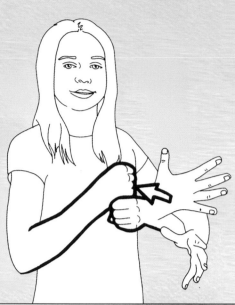

Sam went outside to **get** firewood.

ghost

spirit

The boy was surprised when the **ghost** sat on his lap!

gift

present

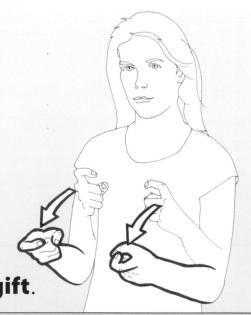

A puppy is a very special birthday **gift**.

giraffe

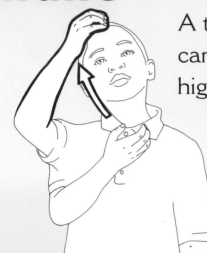

A tall **giraffe** can eat the highest leaves.

girl
female

Gwen likes to dress up like a big **girl**.

give
contribute
contribution
donate
grant

Hawaiians **give** flower wreaths to welcome visitors.

give up
sacrifice
surrender

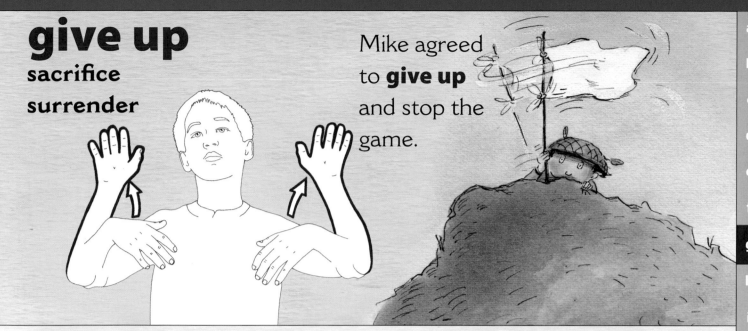

Mike agreed to **give up** and stop the game.

glasses
spectacles

You will see better with those spotted **glasses**.

globe

A **globe** is round to show the shape of Earth.

a b c d e f **g** h i j k l m n o p q r s t u v w x y z

glue

The sticky **glue** spilled all over the table.

go
went

Spot knows he misbehaved and must **go** to the doghouse.

goat

This **goat** has excellent balance.

God

Ancient Greek fishermen prayed to **God** for fish.

gold

A pot of **gold** lies at the end of the rainbow.

gone
**absent
missing**

The safe is empty, and her jewels are **gone**!

a b c d e f g h i j k l m n o p q r s t u v w x y z

good
benevolent
well

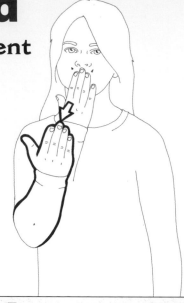

You should be proud of your **good** grades!

good morning

"**Good morning**! It's time to eat breakfast!"

1   **2**

good night

At bedtime, dad came in to say **good night**.

1   **2**

government

The **government** passes laws to protect people.

grandfather
grandpa

Zoey's **Grandfather** George is the father of her dad.

grandmother
grandma
granny

Libby's **grandmother** is the mother of her mom.

grapes

Grapes can taste sour or sweet.

grass
hay

Cutting the **grass** is hard work.

green

Green is the color of summer grass.

group

Every night our family has a **group** hug.

grow

Her bean began to **grow**.

grow up
raise (a child)

Joe wants to **grow up** to be big and strong.

a b c d e f g h i j k l m n o p q r s t u v w x y z

guess

assume
estimate
miss

Can you **guess** how many jelly beans are in the jar?

guide

lead

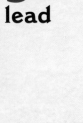

Many blind people have a dog to help **guide** them.

guilty

He felt **guilty** when Mom saw his hand in the cookie jar.

guitar

My uncle plays funny songs on the **guitar**.

gum
chewing gum

A big bubble **gum** burst could be messy.

gym

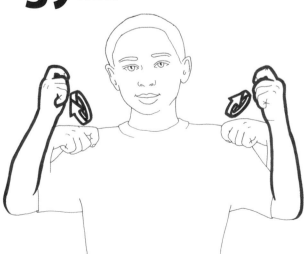

People do different kinds of exercise in a **gym**.

a
b
c
d
e
f
g
h
i
j
k
l
m
n
o
p
q
r
s
t
u
v
w
x
y
z

habit

accustomed
custom
used to

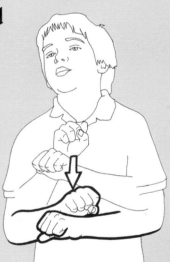

Frisky has a bad **habit** of scratching the furniture.

hair

Nick likes his **hair** long and wild.

hairbrush
brush

A **hairbrush** can help smooth out tangles.

half
one-half

The glass is **half** full.

Halloween

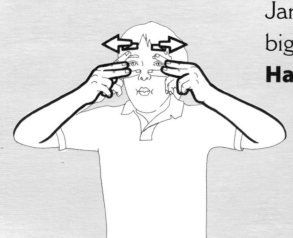

Jared dressed as a big candy corn on **Halloween**.

a b c d e f g h i j k l m n o p q r s t u v w x y z

hamburger
burger

A **hamburger** patty tastes great on a bun.

hands

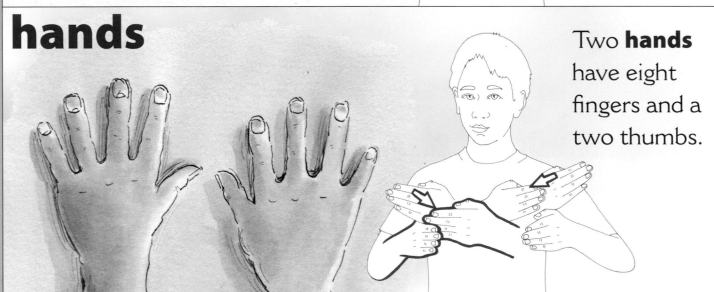

Two **hands** have eight fingers and a two thumbs.

Hanukkah
menorah

Hanukkah is a Jewish holiday in December.

happen

circumstance
coincide
incident
occur

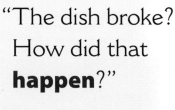

"The dish broke?
How did that
happen?"

happy

cheer
cheerful
content
glad
merry

Spot is excited
and **happy** to play
outside.

hard of hearing

Speak louder for
Grandpa who is
hard of hearing.

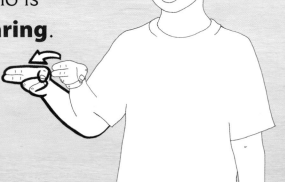

hat

This Mexican **hat** will look good on my head.

hate

abhor
despise
detest
loathe

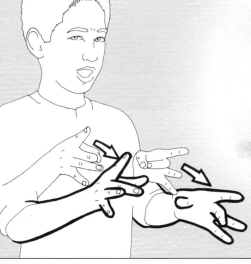

HISSSS

GRRR

Frisky and Spot are angry, but they don't **hate** each other.

have

had
has
own
possess

Farmer ants **have** very busy lives.

ANT FARM

he

her
him
she

Luan can sign that **he** is three years old.

head

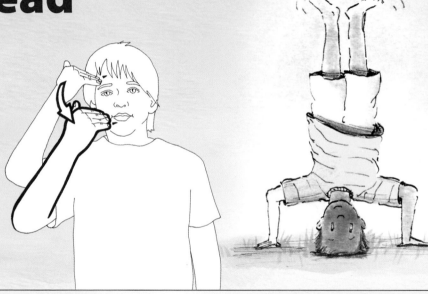

Stand on your **head** and your face will turn red.

health

get well
heal
healthy
well

Eat well and exercise for good **health**.

a b c d e f g h i j k l m n o p q r s t u v w x y z

hearing aid

Not all **hearing aids** look the same.

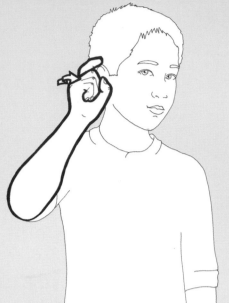

NOTE. The sign for **hearing aid** depends on the type of hearing aid.

heart

The **heart** pumps blood through our bodies.

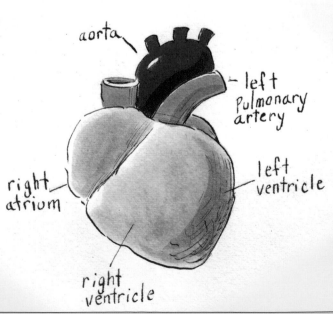

heart
valentine

Show your love with a **heart**-shaped card!

heavy

The weight on the bar is too **heavy** to lift.

helicopter

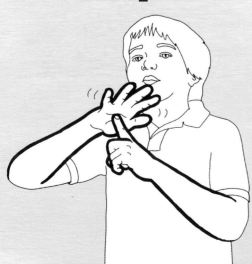

A **helicopter** can fly over our heads and stay there.

a b c d e f g h i j k l m n o p q r s t u v w x y z

hello

hi

wave hello

Saying "**hello**" in different languages is a nice greeting.

help

aid

The lifeguard saved the girl who called for **help**.

her

hers

his

its

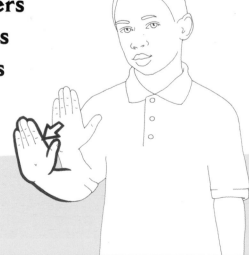

Abby keeps **her** towels separate from Don's towels.

here
present

James said, "**here**," when the teacher called his name.

hide
conceal

He likes to **hide** when it is time to eat peas.

high
altitude

The basket floated **high** up in the sky.

a
b
c
d
e
f
g
h
i
j
k
l
m
n
o
p
q
r
s
t
u
v
w
x
y
z

highway

Cars and trucks drive on a **highway**.

himself
herself
itself

Billy is making a big breakfast by **himself**.

history

History teaches us how people lived in the past.

hit
beat
impact
strike

Jamie swung the bat and **hit** the ball out of the park!

hockey

Ice **hockey** is a fun winter sport.

hold

Hold on a minute and wait until I finish the dishes.

a b c d e f g h i j k l m n o p q r s t u v w x y z

home

The children are happy when Dad comes **home**.

homework

Homework is hard to do when your cat sits on it.

honest
truth
truthful

Bill promised to be **honest** and tell the truth.

hope
anticipate
expect

I **hope** I will win the bike!

WIN A BIKE RAFFLE

horse

A **horse** is an animal you can ride.

hospital
infirmary

GENERAL

EMERGENCY

AMBULANCE

Doctors and nurses help people in the **hospital**.

a b c d e f g h i j k l m n o p q r s t u v w x y z

hot
heat

You need plenty of water in the **hot** desert.

hot dog

I had a **hot dog** in a bun for lunch.

hour

The clock chimes every **hour**.

a
b
c
d
e
f
g
h
i
j
k
l
m
n
o
p
q
r
s
t
u
v
w
x
y
z

house

The **house** stands on a high hill.

how (to do something)

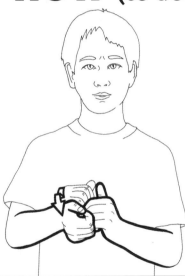

Kate wants to learn **how** to knit a sweater.

how are you?

How are you feeling today?

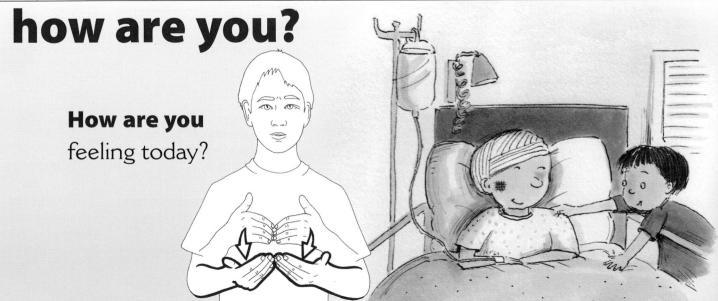

a b c d e f g h i j k l m n o p q r s t u v w x y z

how many?
how much does it cost?

How many muffins will Sally buy?

how much?

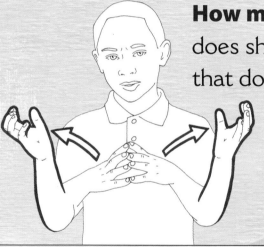

How much does she love that dog?

hug

Bears hold each other close when they **hug**.

a b c d e f g h i j k l m n o p q r s t u v w x y z

hungry

craving
hunger
starving

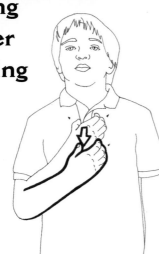

Spot was still **hungry** after eating his dinner.

hurricane

The strong **hurricane** blew away the bike.

hurt

ache
agony
harm
injury
pain
painful
sore

Bobby **hurt** his knee when he fell off the skateboard.

NOTE. **Hurt** is signed on the body part that hurts.

a b c d e f g h i j k l m n o p q r s t u v w x y z

husband

Lucy married the **husband** of her dreams.

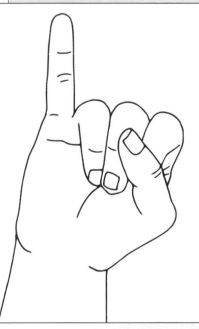

I
me

I am ready to learn how to surf by myself!

ice cream
lollipop

Spot thinks **ice cream** is the best dessert ever.

ice skating
skating

Olive started **ice skating** when she was little.

idea

Inventing the lightbulb was a good **idea**.

a b c d e f g h i j k l m n o p q r s t u v w x y z

a b c d e f g h i j k l m n o p q r s t u v w x y z

if
imagine
suppose

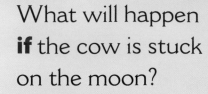

What will happen **if** the cow is stuck on the moon?

ignore

Spot and Kitty often **ignore** each other.

I love you

Joe said, "**I love you**," in a special way.

imagination

Jason uses his **imagination** to make up games.

important

counts
crucial
key
significant
valuable
worth

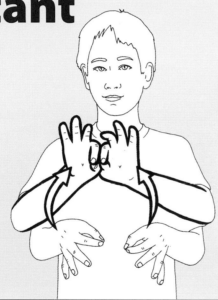

It is **important** to wash your dirty hands with soap.

in

Peas **in** a can taste different than fresh peas.

a b c d e f g h i j k l m n o p q r s t u v w x y z

a b c d e f g h i j k l m n o p q r s t u v w x y z

include

Be sure to **include** all the ingredients.

independence
independent

The United States celebrates its **independence** from England on July 4th.

India

Hindi is the official language of **India**.

Indian
American Indian
Native American

An American **Indian** is also known as a Native American.

international

The **international** center flies flags from many nations.

Internet
network

The **Internet** lets us find information with our computers.

a b c d e f g h i j k l m n o p q r s t u v w x y z

a b c d e f g h i j k l m n o p q r s t u v w x y z

invent
create
make believe
make up

To **invent** the lightbulb, Thomas Edison made his idea work.

investigate
explore

The museum sent him to **investigate** the giant footprint.

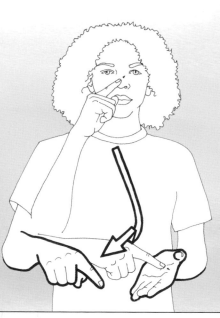

iron

Bert likes to **iron** out the wrinkles in his pants.

island

An **island** is land surrounded by water.

Italy
Italian

The people of **Italy** are proud of their history.

Now, You Know

Deaf people have other ways than flashing the lights to get someone's attention. If two people are close to each other, one will tap the other person's shoulder. If the people are in the same area, they will pound on a table or stomp on the floor. Pounding may seem strange to hearing people, but wood carries vibrations that deaf people can feel, so they look up. Waving is also a good way to make someone notice you. If the person is busy at that moment, she will sign "wait a minute" to let you know that she saw you and will be right with you.

a
b
c
d
e
f
g
h
i
j
k
l
m
n
o
p
q
r
s
t
u
v
w
x
y
z

Jj

jail

People who do crimes go to **jail**.

Japan
Japanese

Tokyo is the capital of **Japan**.

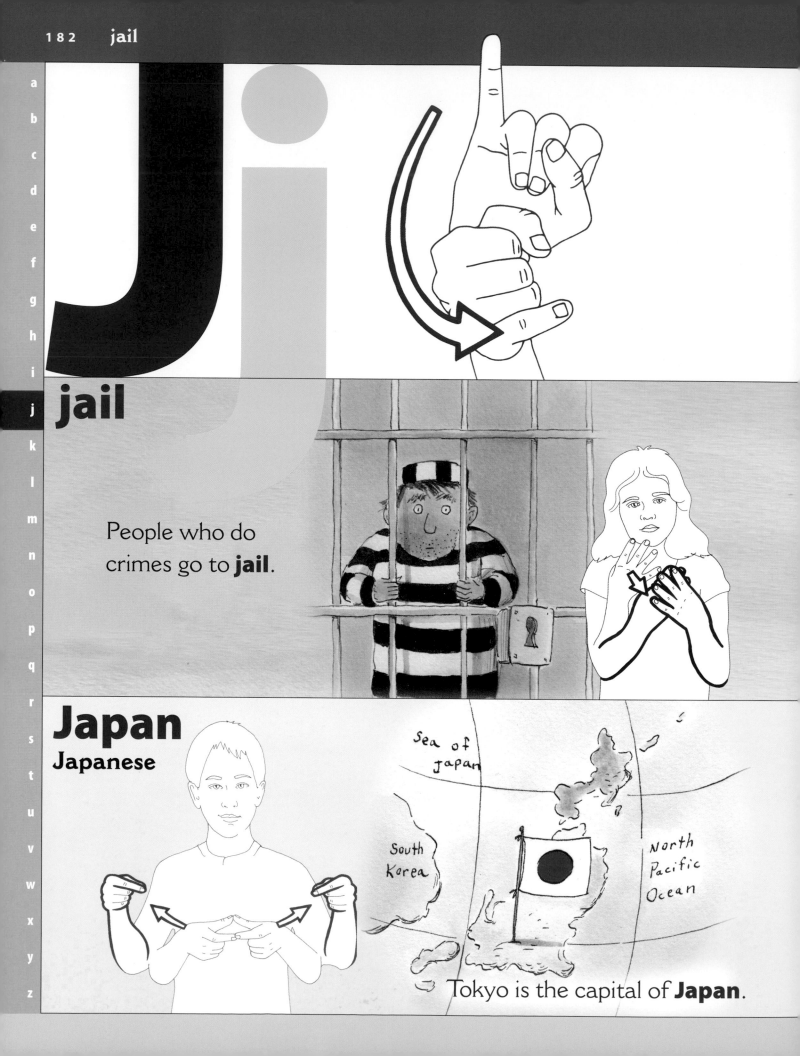

jealous
envious
envy

Peggy is **jealous** of her new baby brother.

jelly
jam

Do you like lots of **jelly** on your toast?

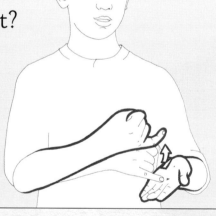

Jesus

Christians believe that **Jesus** is the son of God.

a
b
c
d
e
f
g
h
i
j
k
l
m
n
o
p
q
r
s
t
u
v
w
x
y
z

a
b
c
d
e
f
g
h
i
j
k
l
m
n
o
p
q
r
s
t
u
v
w
x
y
z

Jewish
Judaism

The **Jewish** man wears a traditional prayer shawl.

join
participate

Helen asked Mary to **join** the twirlybird club.

jump

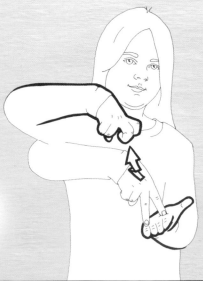

When no one is watching, Spot will **jump** on the trampoline.

jump rope

Rosie likes to **jump rope** for exercise.

kangaroo

Mommy **kangaroo** carries Baby Joey in her pouch.

a b c d e f g h i j k l m n o p q r s t u v w x y z

ketchup
catsup

He always dips his French fries in **ketchup**.

key

Use a **key** to unlock your house.

kick

Soccer players **kick** the ball into the net to score.

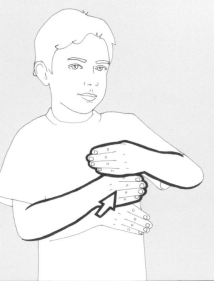

kid

Dad likes to pat his **kid** on the head.

kindergarten

I will start school in **kindergarten**, when I am five.

king

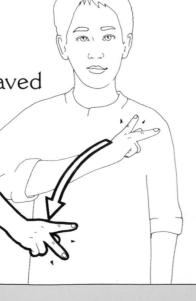

The **king** waved to his loyal subjects.

a b c d e f g h i j **k** l m n o p q r s t u v w x y z

a b c d e f g h i j k l m n o p q r s t u v w x y z

kiss

She gave the frog a **kiss**, and it smiled.

kitchen

Molly loves to cook in her **kitchen**.

kneel

Chad will **kneel** on one knee to hold the football.

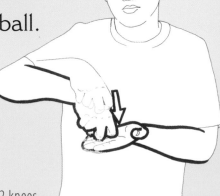

NOTE. You can use 1 or 2 fingers to show 1 or 2 knees.

knife

You can use a **knife** to cut up food.

know

**aware
conscious
familiar
knowledge**

She always seems to **know** when it will rain.

Now, You Know

Many foreign languages include the gender of the subject or object of a sentence in the base form of the word. In Spanish, for example, *hijo* means "male child/son" and *hija* means "female child/daughter." ASL has signs that include gender in the location of the sign. Many of the signs for males are made on or near the forehead—*boy, man, father, brother, uncle, nephew,* and *grandfather*. Signs for females are made on or near the lower cheek—*girl, woman, mother, sister, aunt, niece,* and *grandmother*.

a b c d e f g h i j **k** l m n o p q r s t u v w x y z

L

ladder

Climb a **ladder** to reach the ceiling.

lake

pond

You can go fishing in the **lake**.

land

area
field
property

The farmer grows good food on his **land**.

1   2

language

dialect
tongue

Spot does not understand Baby's **language**.

lap

Kitty purrs when she sits on my **lap**.

a
b
c
d
e
f
g
h
i
j
k
l
m
n
o
p
q
r
s
t
u
v
w
x
y
z

a b c d e f g h i j k **l** m n o p q r s t u v w x y z

laptop computer

Taylor learns to spell on her **laptop computer**.

last
final
lastly

Z is the **last** letter in the alphabet.

late
not yet
tardy
yet

The rabbit worries about being **late** for lunch.

NOTE. Shake your head no when signing **not yet**.

later
after awhile

"Go to your room; we can discuss this at a **later** time."

laugh

If you **laugh** in church, someone might get angry.

law
legal

Spot does not like the **law** against dogs on the beach.

a b c d e f g h i j k **l** m n o p q r s t u v w x y z

lazy

HO HUM....

Doug felt too **lazy** to do any work.

leaf
feather

The bug chews the **leaf** into little bits.

crunch crunch

leap
jump

My Dad and I like to **leap** like a frog!

learn

This student must **learn** how to spell.

leave

abandon
leave it alone
left
leftover
remaining

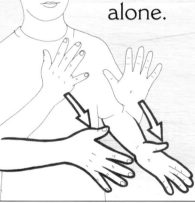

If you see a snake, don't bother it and **leave** it alone.

leave

depart
go away
go out

After the wedding, they will **leave** for their honeymoon.

a b c d e f g h i j k l m n o p q r s t u v w x y z

lecture

address
presentation
sermon
speech
talk

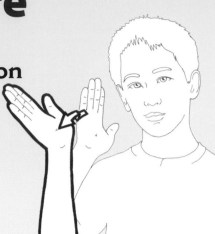

In today's **lecture**, he will talk about dinosaurs.

left (direction)

Did we miss that **left** turn?

leg

The pirate has a wooden **leg** with no foot or toes.

lemon

Mindy used **lemons** to make lemonade.

less

cut back
decrease
lessen

He lost weight when he ate **less** food.

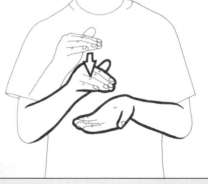

letter

mail

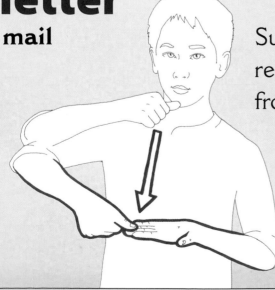

Sue is excited to receive a **letter** from her cousin.

a
b
c
d
e
f
g
h
i
j
k
l
m
n
o
p
q
r
s
t
u
v
w
x
y
z

a
b
c
d
e
f
g
h
i
j
k
l
m
n
o
p
q
r
s
t
u
v
w
x
y
z

lettuce
cabbage

Start making your salad with **lettuce**.

library

A **library** has good books for everyone to borrow.

lie
**falsehood
fib**

The **lie** detector knows when you don't tell the truth.

life
live

Baby birds start their **life** in the nest.

light
lightbulb

The **light** makes it easy to see at night.

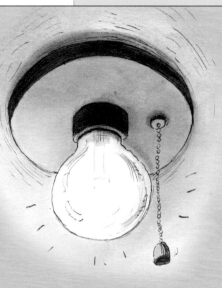

light
lightweight

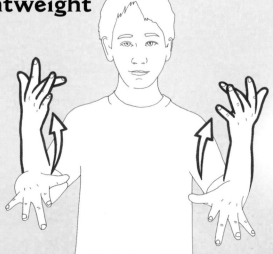

Bobby is too **light** and Jimmy is too heavy to move the seesaw.

a
b
c
d
e
f
g
h
i
j
k
l
m
n
o
p
q
r
s
t
u
v
w
x
y
z

lightning

Long ago some people believed gods threw **lightning**.

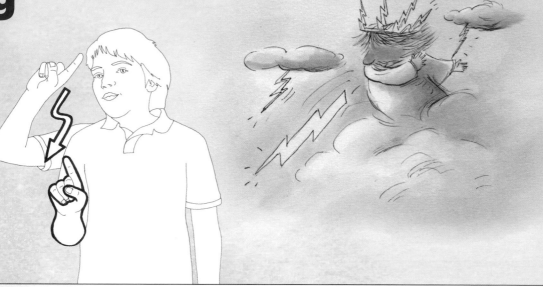

like

Doesn't everybody **like** happy cats?

line

Brianna draws a **line** in the sand.

line up

Students **line up** for class after recess.

lion

The **lion** likes to roar and bite.

lipreading

Lipreading helps you see spoken words on a person's mouth.

AHHH

AHHH

a b c d e f g h i j k l m n o p q r s t u v w x y z

lips
mouth

Rudy licks the ice cream all over his **lips**.

listen
hear

Listen to the rails to hear the train coming.

little
small
tiny

Very **little** things are hard to see.

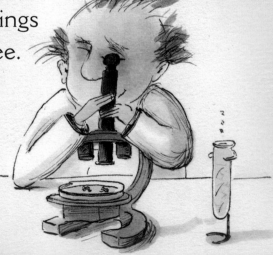

live
alive
dwell
life
survive

Native Americans used to **live** in teepees.

lobster
crabs

A **lobster** has two big red claws.

lock
lock up

Lock up your bicycle to keep it safe.

lonely
lonesome

This **lonely** fish needs a friend.

long
length

They spent the afternoon taking a **long** walk.

long ago
ancient
long time ago
used to

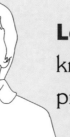

Long ago, knights protected cities.

look

Let's **look** at the map to see our exact location.

lose (competition)
lost

She felt sad to **lose** the contest.

lose (object)
loss
lost

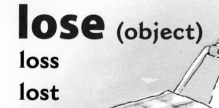

If mommy does not stop, Sam will **lose** his bear.

a
b
c
d
e
f
g
h
i
j
k
l
m
n
o
p
q
r
s
t
u
v
w
x
y
z

loud

The baby gave a **loud** cry after she was born.

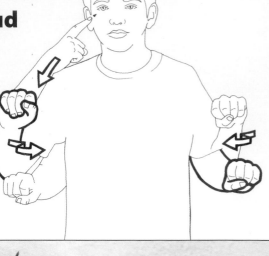

love

Cats in **love** make a heart with their tails.

low

Ryan wondered how **low** he could go.

lucky
luck

Finding a four-leaf clover is very **lucky**!

lunch

He eats **lunch** in the middle of his day.

NOTE. **Lunch** can be signed two different ways.

a
b
c
d
e
f
g
h
i
j
k
l
m
n
o
p
q
r
s
t
u
v
w
x
y
z

machine

engine
factory
mechanism
plant

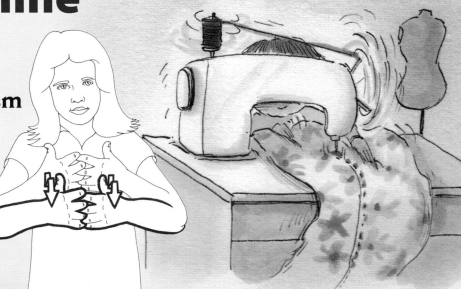

Ruby makes nice dresses on her sewing **machine**.

magazine

brochure
catalog
pamphlet

Magazines have lots of pictures and short stories.

magic

Spot surprised everyone with his **magic** trick.

make
manufacture
produce

What did you **make** in art class today?

man
guy
male

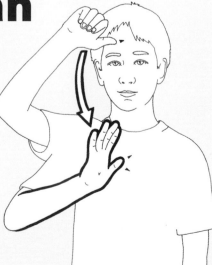

This little **man** has a big club to protect himself.

a b c d e f g h i j k l **m** n o p q r s t u v w x y z

many
lots

numerous

The jester juggles **many** balls at once.

mask

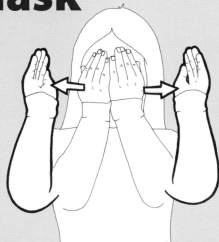

She glued a pointy yellow nose on the **mask**.

math
mathematics

We learn how to add and subtract in **math** class.

maybe

might
perhaps
probably

Maybe I could make a suggestion?

mean

cruel
harsh
rude
unkind

It is **mean** to pull someone's hair.

mean

intend
purpose

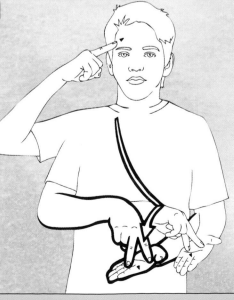

This symbol **means** beauty.

a b c d e f g h i j k l m n o p q r s t u v w x y z

measure
inches
miles
size

Spot does not want Luis to **measure** his plump tummy.

meat
beef
content
flesh
steak
substance

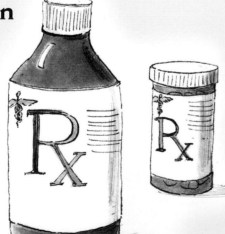

The butcher sells many kinds of **meat**.

medicine
poison

Take **medicine** only when you are sick.

meet

The little green man was shocked to **meet** Betty.

meeting
convention
session

This week, the club **meeting** is in Tyler's backyard.

merry go round
carnival
fair

Let's ride the **merry go round!**

a
b
c
d
e
f
g
h
i
j
k
l
m
n
o
p
q
r
s
t
u
v
w
x
y
z

mess

Judy made a **mess** with the paints.

Mexico

Mexico is the first country below the United States.

microwave

A **microwave** can heat food fast.

midnight

On New Year's Eve, he fell asleep before 12:00 **midnight**.

milk

Most kids like to drink a lot of **milk**.

minute

moment

Your time in the race was one **minute** flat.

a
b
c
d
e
f
g
h
i
j
k
l
m
n
o
p
q
r
s
t
u
v
w
x
y
z

mirror

A curvy **mirror** can make you look odd.

mistake
error

She made a big **mistake** on that sleeve.

misunderstand

When you **misunderstand** the directions, you do the wrong thing.

Monday

The school week starts on **Monday** with frowns and yawns!

money
funds

We use **money** to buy things.

monkey
ape
chimpanzee
gorilla

The **monkey** enjoys swinging in the trees.

a b c d e f g h i j k l **m** n o p q r s t u v w x y z

a b c d e f g h i j k l **m** n o p q r s t u v w x y z

month

January is the first **month** of the year.

NOTE. To sign **monthly**, repeat **month**.

moon

A full **moon** can light up the night sky.

more

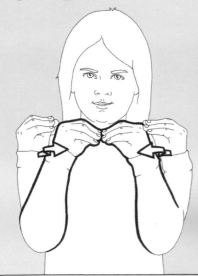

I'm still hungry, **more** corn please!

morning
A.M.

He woke up early to watch the **morning** sun rise.

most

If you earn the **most** points, you win!

1,250   113   1,249

mother
mama
mom
mommy

The **mother** pig loves her little piglets.

a b c d e f g h i j k l **m** n o p q r s t u v w x y z

a
b
c
d
e
f
g
h
i
j
k
l
m
n
o
p
q
r
s
t
u
v
w
x
y
z

motorcycle
moped
snowmobile

She rides her **motorcycle** to work.

mountain

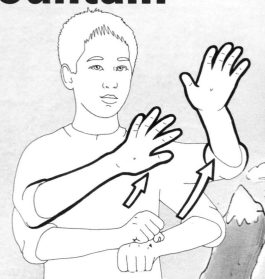

Jesse is tired from climbing the **mountain**.

mouse

The **mouse** devoured the biscuit it found on the floor.

move

You need help when you **move** to a new home.

movie
cinema
film

People like to watch a scary **movie** on a big screen.

multiply
figure out

In math, we **multiply** to add faster.

museum

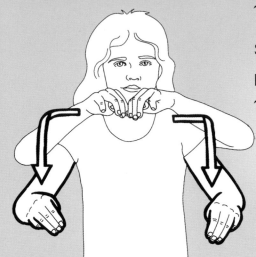

The dinosaur skeleton in the **museum** scared Tommy.

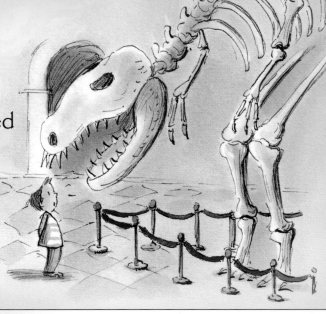

music
sing
song

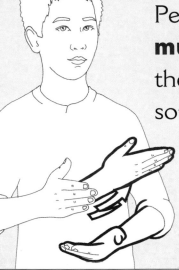

People listen to **music** to enjoy the pleasant sounds.

must
should

Children **must** be this tall to ride.

a b c d e f g h i j k l **m** n o p q r s t u v w x y z

my
mine

My kitty likes the way I hug her.

myself

I made my bed all by **myself**.

NOTE. **Myself** can be signed two different ways.

a b c d e f g h i j k l **m** n o p q r s t u v w x y z

Nn

name

The parrot's **name** is Handsome.

near
close
nearby

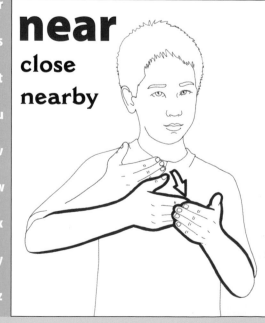

They stretch **near** each other, but they don't touch.

neck

Nefertidi had a very long **neck**.

need

have to
necessary
needs
need to
ought to
supposed to

I think we **need** another oar.

neighbor

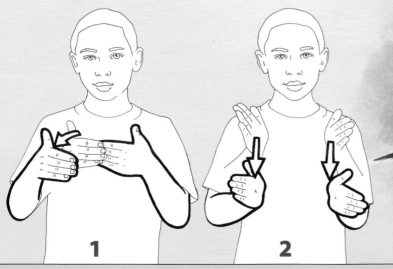

1

2

A good **neighbor** can be a close friend for life.

a b c d e f g h i j k l m n o p q r s t u v w x y z

never

AND I'M NEVER COMING back!

When he ran away, he said, "I'm **never** coming back."

new
fresh

Suzy rode her **new** tricycle right away.

newspaper
print

People read a **newspaper** every day to learn what is happening.

New York

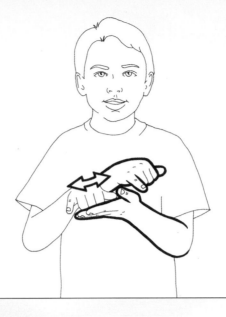

New York is known as the Empire State.

nickel

five cents

You can trade a **nickel** for five pennies.

night

P.M.

The full moon illuminated the **night** sky.

a
b
c
d
e
f
g
h
i
j
k
l
m
n
o
p
q
r
s
t
u
v
w
x
y
z

no

When Jenna asked to keep the kittens, Mama said **no**.

noise
noisy

Folks make lots of loud **noise** on New Year's Eve.

none
nothing

At the Easter egg hunt, Billy found **none**.

noon
twelve o'clock

Otto eats lunch every day at **noon**.

north

The weather vane pointed **north**.

nose

Mr. P's **nose** still looked big in the mirror.

a b c d e f g h i j k l m n o p q r s t u v w x y z

now

Please clean your room **now**, before it explodes!

number

Bowling shoes have a **number** on them.

nurse

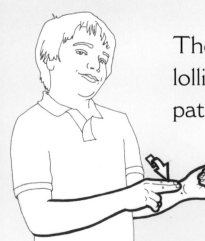

The **nurse** gives lollipops to tiny patients.

nuts
peanuts

Nuts are a
healthy snack.

Oo

ocean

Many different fish
and water animals live
in the **ocean**.

a b c d e f g h i j k l m n **o** p q r s t u v w x y z

off

The teddy bear fell **off** Sam's lap.

okay

Are you feeling **okay**?

old
age

Grandpa Dog looks **old** but feels young.

Olympics

Athletes from around the world go to the **Olympics**.

on

on top of
upon

The bows **on** the Christmas presents were pretty.

once

one time

He needed to putt only **once** to win the tournament!

a b c d e f g h i j k l m n o p q r s t u v w x y z

a b c d e f g h i j k l m n **o** p q r s t u v w x y z

once in a while
occasionally

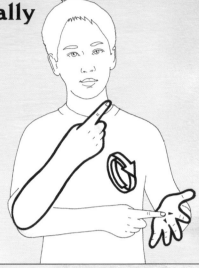
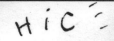

Once in a while, not often, Spot gets the hiccups.

onion

Slicing an **onion** can make you cry.

open

The store will **open** in a few minutes.

open (a book)

Kate wants to **open** her sister's diary and read it.

open a door

When Daddy **opens the door**, we all run to hug him.

open a window

He will **open the window** to let in some air.

opposite
contrary

contrast

Round Paul loves his **opposite**, Slender Sal.

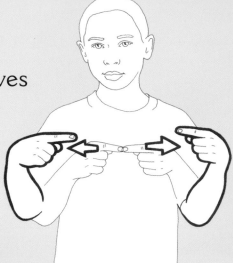

orange

An **orange** is a juicy, round fruit.

NOTE. This sign is used for the color and the fruit.

other
another

else

One sock has polka dots and the **other** has stripes.

our
ours

Our family has won many swimming races.

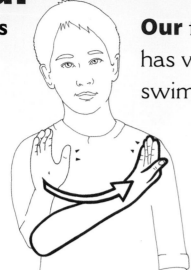

ourselves

We grow our vegetables **ourselves**.

out
outdoors
outside

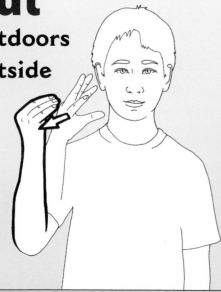

"We have been inside too long—let's go **out** and play!"

owl

An **owl** hunts for food at night.

Pp

page

You read a book one **page** at a time.

paint

How did I **paint** myself into a corner?

pancake

The top **pancake** gets the most syrup.

pants
**jeans
slacks
trousers**

Pants come in lots of shapes and colors.

a b c d e f g h i j k l m n o **p** q r s t u v w x y z

paper

Folding **paper** cranes is a popular origami technique.

parents

These **parents** love their baby.

party

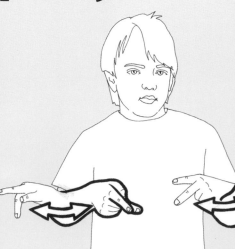

Everyone likes to go to a costume **party**.

past

ago
a while ago
back
before
previous
previously
was
were

Books teach us what happened in the **past**.

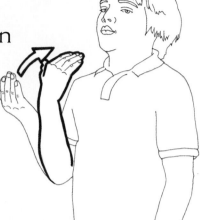

patient

bear
patience
put up with
stand
take
tolerate

An ice fisherman must be **patient** and wait a long time.

patient (medical)

The doctor checks the ear of his young **patient**.

pay
payment

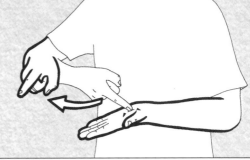

You must **pay** for a ticket to see the movie.

peach

A **peach** has fuzzy skin on the outside.

NOTE. This sign is used for the color and the fruit.

pear

A **pear** is a delicious fruit when it is ripe.

peas

Peas are an excellent green vegetable.

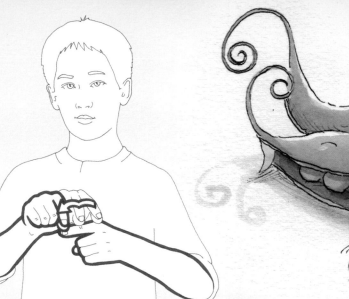

pen

Use a **pen** to write or draw in ink.

pencil

If you make a mistake with a **pencil**, you can erase it.

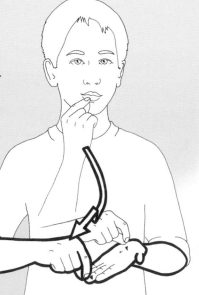

a b c d e f g h i j k l m n o p q r s t u v w x y z

penguin

The **penguin** is floating on ice.

penny
cent
one cent

A **penny** is worth one cent.

people

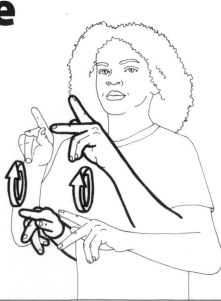

People come in all shapes and sizes.

pepper

People use **pepper** to flavor their food.

perfect

accurate
exact
perfection
specific

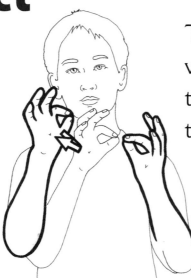

The bath water was the **perfect** temperature.

person

How did one **person** plant all the apple seeds?

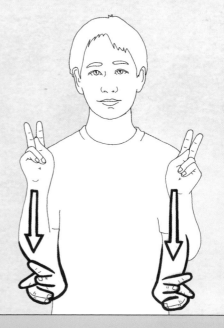

a b c d e f g h i j k l m n o **p** q r s t u v w x y z

a b c d e f g h i j k l m n o **p** q r s t u v w x y z

pet
spoiled person

Adopting a **pet** made him very happy.

piano

Ben practices every day to make beautiful music on the **piano**.

picnic

Who will eat the last hot dog at the **picnic**?

picture
image
photograph

The safe is hidden behind the **picture**.

pie

Cherry **pie** tastes great for dessert.

pig
hog
pork

The **pig** puts butter and salt on corn on the cob.

a b c d e f g h i j k l m n o **p** q r s t u v w x y z

a b c d e f g h i j k l m n o **p** q r s t u v w x y z

pillow

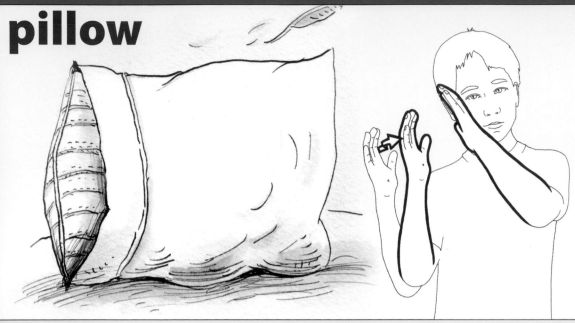

Rest your head on a **pillow** and sleep well.

pills
tablets

Pills help you get better when you are sick.

pilot

The **pilot** waves as she flies away.

1   **2**

pink

Her **pink** hair looks like cotton candy!

pizza

Pizza is my favorite food.

place
location
position
site

Holland is the **place** to see many windmills.

a
b
c
d
e
f
g
h
i
j
k
l
m
n
o
p
q
r
s
t
u
v
w
x
y
z

plan
organize

I drew you a new floor **plan** for my room.

plate
dish

saucer

He always cleans his **plate**.

play
party

recess

Kids need time to go out and **play**.

please

May I have some ice cream **please**?

pocket

The mouse fits comfortably in the shirt **pocket**.

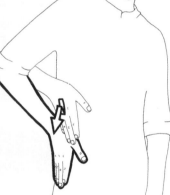

police
cop
officer
sheriff

This **police** officer is directing traffic.

a b c d e f g h i j k l m n o p q r s t u v w x y z

a b c d e f g h i j k l m n o **p** q r s t u v w x y z

polite
courteous
well behaved
well mannered

The **polite** waiter is nice to his customers.

poor
destitute
impoverished

He was **poor** with no money, but happy anyway.

popcorn

Popcorn is the perfect snack.

possible

able

capable

possibly

Is it **possible** we could ever be friends?

poster

bulletin board

notice

sign

Her Earth Day sign won first place in the **poster** contest.

potato

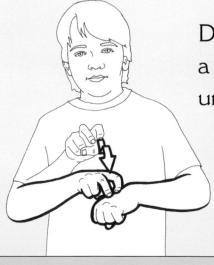

Did you know a **potato** grows underground?

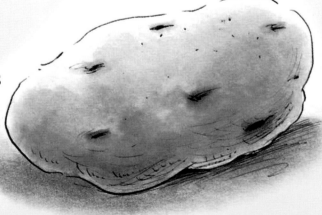

a b c d e f g h i j k l m n o p q r s t u v w x y z

pour

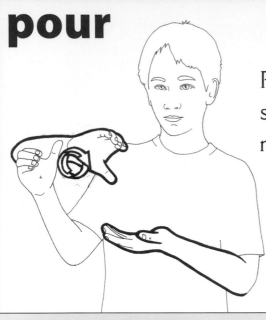

Please **pour** some milk in my tea.

practice
drill
exercise
rehearse

I **practice** every day to play better.

pray
prayer

Every night, the cat would **pray** for a fish dinner.

president
superintendent

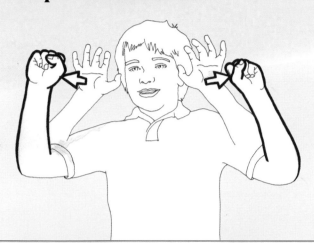

Can you name each **president** on Mt. Rushmore?

prince

Prince Robb is the king's son.

princess

Prince Robb's sister, **Princess** Ella, does not like peas.

a
b
c
d
e
f
g
h
i
j
k
l
m
n
o
p
q
r
s
t
u
v
w
x
y
z

program

I hope you enjoy tonight's **program** of speakers.

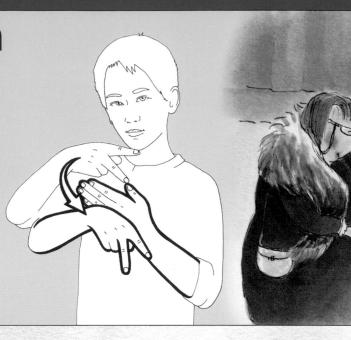

promise

commit
dedicate
obligate
obligation
pledge

PINKY SWEAR

They made a **promise** to be best friends forever.

pull
draw out

Spot has to **pull** Ryan.

pumpkin

He carved the **pumpkin** for Halloween.

purple

This medal is the color **purple**.

push
shove

It isn't easy to **push** a cart with a flat tire.

put
place

Oscar is big enough to **put** the toothbrush back on the sink.

puzzle
jigsaw puzzle

This **puzzle** is almost finished!

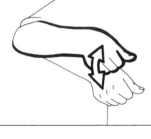

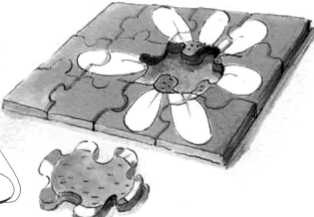

Now, You Know

We've all been told that it's not polite to point, but pointing has an important function in ASL. In a conversation, a signer can mention a person by fingerspelling his name and then pointing to a specific place. After that, every time the signer points to that place, it means "he." This also works for objects to mean "it."

quarter

twenty-five cents

A **quarter** is worth 25 cents.

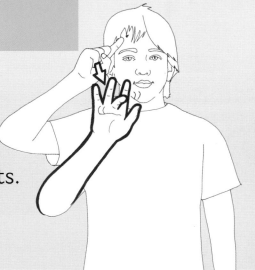

queen

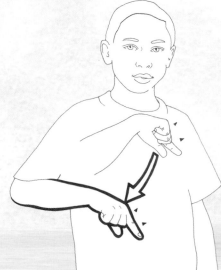

The **queen** has many worker bees.

question

He raised his hand to ask a **question**.

quiet
**peaceful
silence
silent
still**

She told us to be **quiet** in the library.

quit
drop out

Don't **quit** now!
Keep going.

quote

idiom
quotation
subject
theme
title
topic

To **quote** Ben Franklin, write his exact words.

Rr

rabbit

bunny

A **rabbit** has long, floppy ears.

a
b
c
d
e
f
g
h
i
j
k
l
m
n
o
p
q
r
s
t
u
v
w
x
y
z

raccoon

The **raccoon** likes to sneak around at night.

radio

What song is playing on the **radio**?

rain

Rain, rain, go away! I don't want to get wet!

rainbow

Can you name all the colors of the **rainbow**?

read

They **read** the newspaper at the same time.

ready

Joe is always **ready** to eat.

a b c d e f g h i j k l m n o p q **r** s t u v w x y z

red

A **red** light means stop.

refrigerator

The **refrigerator** has plenty of midnight snacks.

regular

ordinary
proper
usual

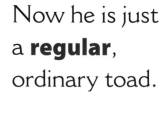

Now he is just a **regular**, ordinary toad.

relax
relaxed
rest

Vacation is a time to **relax**.

religion
religious

Each **religion** has a different symbol.

remember
recall
recollect

She can't **remember** why she tied a bow on her finger.

a b c d e f g h i j k l m n o p q **r** s t u v w x y z

residential school

institute
institution
school for the deaf

Some deaf children go to a **residential school** instead of public school.

restaurant

Dad ordered lobster for dinner at the **restaurant**.

restroom

Always make sure you go in the right **restroom**.

rich
prosperous
wealth
wealthy

Liam has so much money, he is **rich**.

ride (in a vehicle)

Dogs love to **ride** in cars!

ride (on an animal)

Some kids prefer to **ride** pigs.

right (direction)

Use your left arm to signal a **right** turn.

river

They floated down the **river** between two towns.

road

avenue
lane
method
path
street
trail
way

Why did the chicken cross the **road**?

rock
stone

The ant carried the **rock** home.

rocket
missile
space shuttle

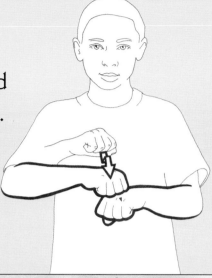

The **rocket** launched high into the sky.

roller blading

Roller blading is tricky with only one skinny line of wheels on the skates.

roller skating
skating

Roller skating is easy with two rows of wheels on my skates.

roof

The **roof** over his head keeps him dry.

room

The janitor keeps mops, brooms, and cleaning supplies in one **room**.

rooster

At dawn the **rooster** crows.

rope

A **rope** is much stronger than string.

rose

Is that **rose** for me?!

a b c d e f g h i j k l m n o p q r s t u v w x y z

a b c d e f g h i j k l m n o p q r s t u v w x y z

rub
scrub

First **rub** with soap, then rinse with water.

rule
principle
regulation

The restaurant has a **rule** about wearing shoes.

run
in a hurry

The mouse likes to **run** for exercise.

runny nose

You need a lot of tissues when you have a **runny nose**.

Russia
Russian

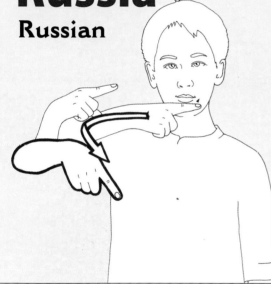

Russia is the largest country in the world.

Now, You Know

Alexander Graham Bell invented the telephone in 1876, but deaf people could not use it until 1964. That was the year when three deaf men invented a way for deaf people to type to each other over the phone lines. They created a TDD (telecommunications device for the deaf). Technology has changed a lot since the mid-1960s, and today new equipment like the webcam lets deaf people see and sign to each other. Many people, both deaf and hearing, use Skype and videophones to communicate with each other. Deaf people can even call hearing people by using a video relay service.

S s

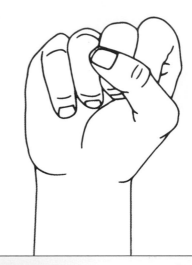

sad
mournful
tragic
unhappy

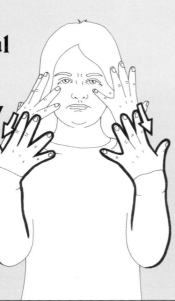

Dropping ice cream on the ground is so **sad**!

salad

A good **salad** includes lettuce, tomatoes, and carrots.

salt

A little **salt** adds flavor to food.

same

alike
also
in common
like
mutual
similar

The twins are dressed in the **same** clothes.

sandals

flip flops

Sandals are the best beach shoes.

a b c d e f g h i j k l m n o p q r s t u v w x y z

sandwich

picnic

My favorite lunch is a bologna and cheese **sandwich**.

Santa Claus

Santa Claus brought us a bag full of gifts.

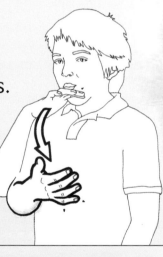

Saturday

Last **Saturday** we washed the car.

sauce
salad dressing
syrup

Salad dressing is one type of **sauce**.

save
keep
preserve

Save your piggy bank until it is full.

school

Some kids wear uniforms to **school**.

science

Science is his favorite class.

scissors
clippers

Scissors are sharp, so be careful and don't cut yourself.

search
explore
look for
seek

Mom told Bobby to **search** for his shoe under his bed.

a b c d e f g h i j k l m n o p q r s t u v w x y z

second (time unit)

There are 60 **seconds** in one minute.

secret

confidential
password
personal
private

The chef never tells anyone his **secret** recipes.

see

eyesight
sight
vision

Without glasses, she can't **see** the last line on the chart.

a
b
c
d
e
f
g
h
i
j
k
l
m
n
o
p
q
r
s
t
u
v
w
x
y
z

a b c d e f g h i j k l m n o p q r s t u v w x y z

send
mail

Amy likes to **send** letters to her cousin.

sentence
statement

Sam's punishment for cheating was to write a **sentence** fifty times.

I will not cheat again.
I will not cheat again
I will not cheat.

serve
minister to
service
wait on

Mr. Mouse was happy to **serve** Kitty breakfast in bed.

set up
base
erect
establish
found

They **set up** a garden club on the farm.

sew
sewing

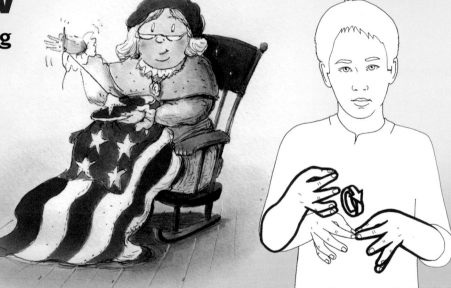

Everyone should learn to **sew.**

shampoo

Shampoo makes your hair nice and clean.

share
average
mean

They always share **popcorn** at the movies.

sheep

A **sheep** is such a fluffy animal.

shelf
mantle

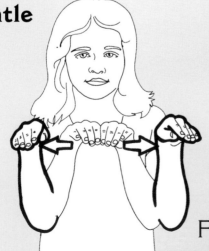

Fran puts her bowling trophies on the **shelf**.

a b c d e f g h i j k l m n o p q r s t u v w x y z

shine
bright
glow
shining
shiny

The tea set had a glossy **shine**.

shirt
top

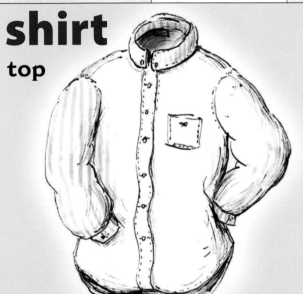

This **shirt** has buttons and a collar.

shoes

Which **shoes** are your favorite to wear?

a
b
c
d
e
f
g
h
i
j
k
l
m
n
o
p
q
r
s
t
u
v
w
x
y
z

short (height)
small

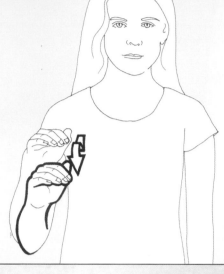

She is too **short** to reach the top shelf.

shorts

These **shorts** are perfect to wear for mountain climbing.

show
demonstrate
example
model
reveal
sample

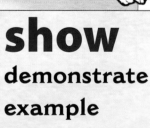

Let me **show** you how it's done.

shy
bashful

The **shy** dog is afraid of new dogs.

sick
disease
ill
illness
sickness

Being **sick** with a cold is no fun.

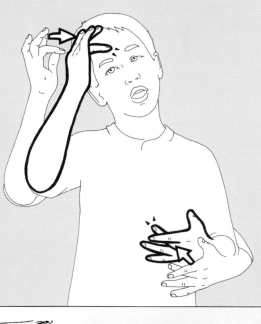

side

One **side** of the building is painted green.

a
b
c
d
e
f
g
h
i
j
k
l
m
n
o
p
q
r
s
t
u
v
w
x
y
z

silly

This Halloween costume looks **silly**.

sing
hymn
song

Everyone loves to hear her **sing**.

sister

She walked her little **sister** home from a party.

sit
sit down

After a busy day, it feels good to **sit** down.

skateboard

You can travel fast on a **skateboard**.

skeleton
bones

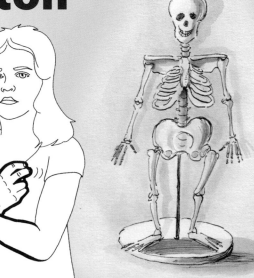

A human **skeleton** has more than 200 bones!

a b c d e f g h i j k l m n o p q r s t u v w x y z

skin

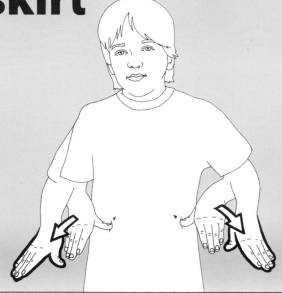

The beekeeper has to cover all of his **skin**.

skirt

Her favorite **skirt** is bright red.

skunk

Would you kiss this smelly **skunk**?

sky

The kite flies high in the **sky**.

sleep

Sometimes Max walks in his **sleep**.

slippers

The fuzzy bunny **slippers** are so cozy!

a b c d e f g h i j k l m n o p q r s t u v w x y z

a b c d e f g h i j k l m n o p q r s t u v w x y z

slow
slowly

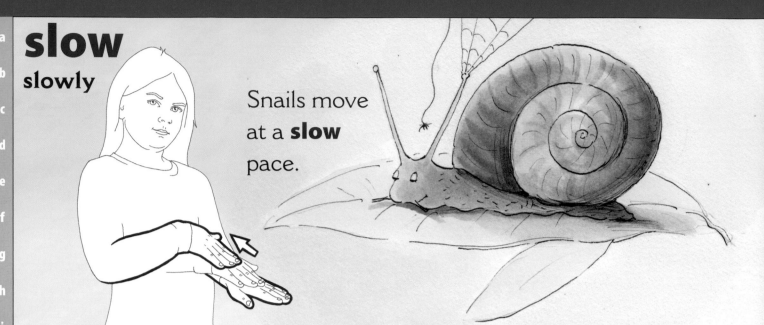

Snails move at a **slow** pace.

smart
bright
clever
intellect
intelligence
intelligent
sharp

This math book is for **smart** babies.

smell
fragrance
odor
scent

The skunk coat and hat **smell** strange.

smile
grin

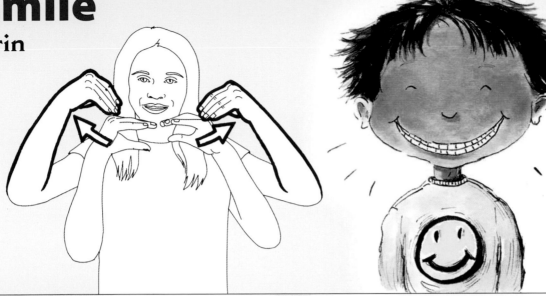

Show me your best **smile**!

smoke

Fire creates **smoke**.

snake

The **snake** wrapped around the tree branch.

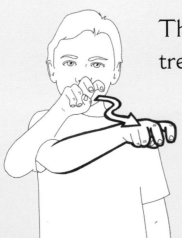

snow

They played in the **snow** all day.

snowboarding

Let's go **snowboarding** in the mountains!

soap

Use the **soap** to
clean your hands.

soccer

The friends played **soccer** after school.

social studies

Landon learned about ancient Egypt in **social studies** class.

socks

These **socks** keep my feet warm.

a b c d e f g h i j k l m n o p q r s t u v w x y z

soda
Coke
pop

Soda is a sweet and bubbly drink.

sofa
couch

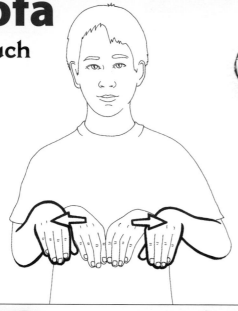

The comfy **sofa** is the perfect place to nap.

soft

The rabbit's fur feels so **soft** to touch!

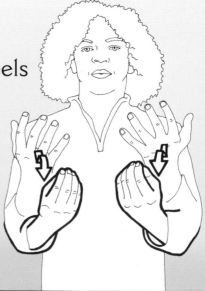

a b c d e f g h i j k l m n o p q r s t u v w x y z

solid

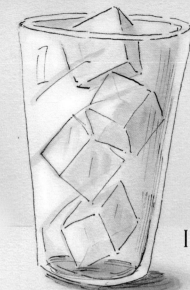

Ice is **solid** water.

some

part
piece
portion
section

He saved **some** of his allowance every week.

sometimes

every so often
once in a while
periodically
seldom

Sometimes, but not always, my daddy gives me a piggyback ride.

a
b
c
d
e
f
g
h
i
j
k
l
m
n
o
p
q
r
s
t
u
v
w
x
y
z

a
b
c
d
e
f
g
h
i
j
k
l
m
n
o
p
q
r
s
t
u
v
w
x
y
z

son

This dad brings his **son** to all his baseball games.

soon
shortly

Squirrel must collect acorns now because winter is coming **soon**.

sorry
apologize
apology
pardon
regret

I'm **sorry** I broke your flower pot.

sour

bitter
lemon
tart

This lemonade tastes **sour**.

south

southern

The compass is pointing **south**.

spaghetti

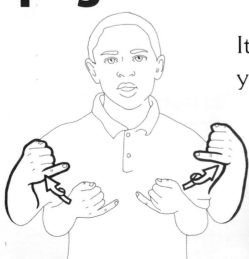

It is not polite to slurp your **spaghetti**.

Spain

Bullfighting is a famous tradition in **Spain**.

speak

Actors must **speak** their words clearly in a play.

special
except unique

"Starry Night" is a **special** painting.

speech
speechreading

Dwayne practiced saying words with the **speech** therapist.

spider

This **spider** has eight legs.

spoon
soup

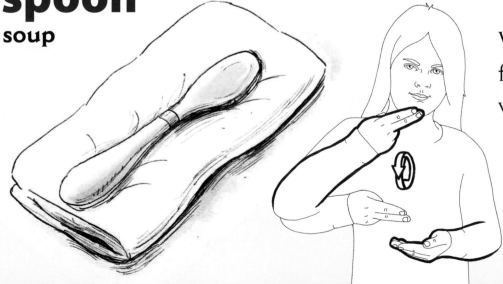

What kinds of food can you eat with a **spoon**?

sports

athletics
competition
contest
race
run

Our family loves **sports**.

spread

distribute

scatter

Lava from the volcano **spread** all through the land.

spring

plants

In **spring**, flowers attract bees and butterflies.

square

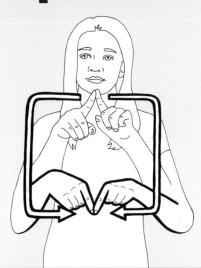

A **square** has four equal sides.

squirrel

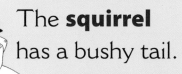

The **squirrel** has a bushy tail.

stairs
flight of steps

The **stairs** go up to my room.

stamps
postage stamps

We use **stamps** to mail letters.

stand

The doorman must **stand** very still.

stars

The night sky is full of **stars**.

stay
remain

Tim can't go out for recess—he must **stay** in the classroom.

steal
rob

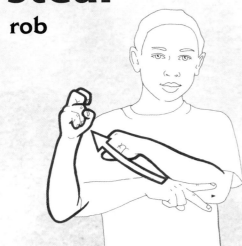

It is wrong to **steal** someone's wallet.

step

Take one **step** forward, then two steps back.

a
b
c
d
e
f
g
h
i
j
k
l
m
n
o
p
q
r
s
t
u
v
w
x
y
z

stomach
gut
intuition

My **stomach** gets big when I eat too much food.

stop
cease

Cars must **stop** and wait for children to cross the street.

store
shop

Our hardware **store** has everything you need to buy!

story
fable
parable
tale

Daddy reads me a **story** every night.

straight

Use a ruler to draw a **straight** line.

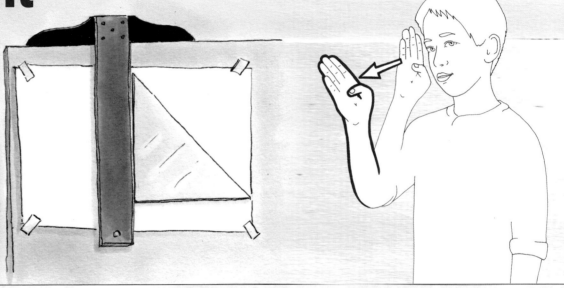

strange
funny
odd
peculiar
weird

This isn't a normal island; it feels **strange**.

a
b
c
d
e
f
g
h
i
j
k
l
m
n
o
p
q
r
s
t
u
v
w
x
y
z

strawberry

This **strawberry** tastes sweet.

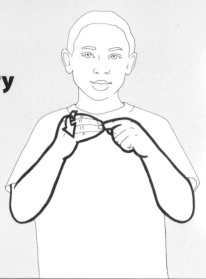

strong
brave
confidence
courageous
might
mighty
strength

POKE

Your muscles feel really **strong**!

student
pupil

The **student** was excited for the first day of school.

I ♥ SCHOOL

1

2

study

If you **study** hard, you will do well in school.

submarine

The **submarine** travels underwater through the ocean.

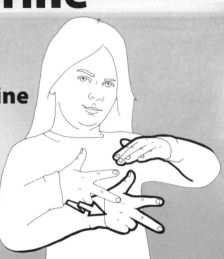

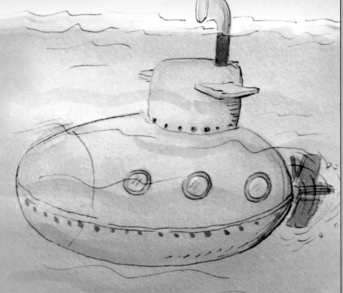

subtract

minus

subtraction

If you **subtract** 4 from 13, you get 9.

summary
abbreviate
condense
summarize

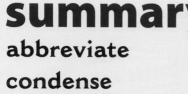

His **summary** of the accident briefly explained what happened.

summer

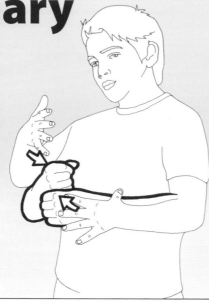

Every June, Zack gets ready for **summer** fun.

sun
sunlight

The **sun** is very hot and bright.

Sunday

The candy store is closed on **Sunday**.

surprise

amazement
astonishment
suddenly
surprised

Julie made breakfast as a
surprise for her mom.

sweep

broom

Use a broom to
sweep the floors.

sweet
sugar

Sugar makes hot chocolate taste **sweet**.

swim
swimming

Penny has **swim** practice every morning before school.

swing

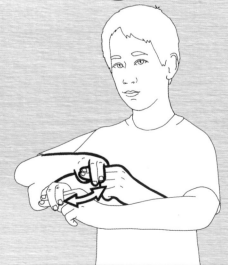

It's fun to **swing** to and fro!

Tt

take
took

Would you like to **take** a cupcake?

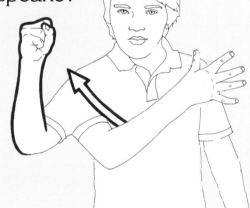

talk
**converse
dialogue**

MA MA?

DA DA
DA DA

Baby is
learning to
talk.

a b c d e f g h i j k l m n o p q r s **t** u v w x y z

a b c d e f g h i j k l m n o p q r s **t** u v w x y z

tall (object)

This candlestick is too **tall** to jump over.

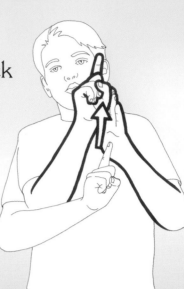

tall (person)

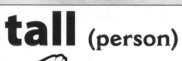

Basketball players are very **tall**.

tan

The zookeeper's uniform is the color **tan**.

tape
scotch tape

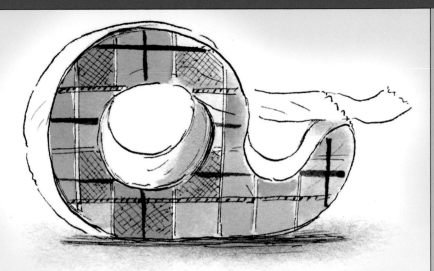

Tape can fix torn paper.

tea

Would you like a cup of **tea**?

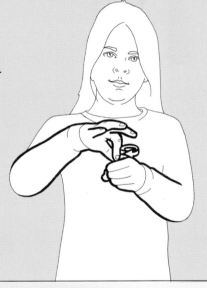

teach
educate
instruct

Grandpa will **teach** me to play golf.

teacher

educator
instructor
professor

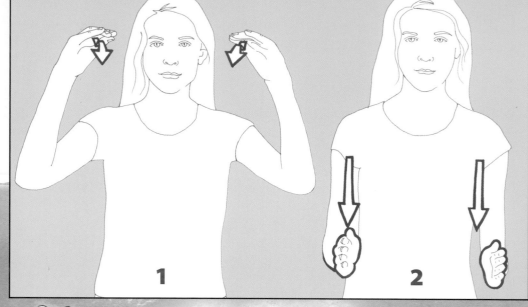

1 2

Our math **teacher** makes learning fun.

team

We have only one girl on the **team**.

tease
joke
kid

When you **tease** me, it hurts my feelings.

teeth

Grandpa cleans his **teeth** every night.

telephone
phone

Alexander Graham Bell invented the **telephone**.

It's for you again Watson....

a b c d e f g h i j k l m n o p q r s **t** u v w x y z

a
b
c
d
e
f
g
h
i
j
k
l
m
n
o
p
q
r
s
t
u
v
w
x
y
z

tell
reveal

I have important news to **tell** you.

tell me

Please **tell me** where the bathroom is.

temperature
fever

The sick dog had a high **temperature**.

tennis

Spot plays **tennis** every weekend.

tent
camping

When we go camping, we sleep in a **tent**.

test
exam
examination
quiz

He was nervous during the math **test**.

Test Today

a b c d e f g h i j k l m n o p q r s t u v w x y z

Thanksgiving

Eating turkey on **Thanksgiving** is an American custom.

thank you
thank
thanks

Bowing can mean **thank you** in Japan.

theater
drama
performance
play
show

We went to the **theater** to see a play.

their

Their son plays tuba in the band.

themselves

They baked the cake all by **themselves**.

there

There she is!

a b c d e f g h i j k l m n o p q r s **t** u v w x y z

these

These roses won first place at the flower show.

they
them

They decided to arm wrestle.

thick

The rhino read every word in the **thick** book.

thin

The stray dog is very **thin**.

things
objects

He put many interesting **things** in his backpack.

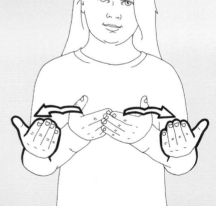

think
sense
thought

Always **think** in your mind to solve a problem.

a b c d e f g h i j k l m n o p q r s t u v w x y z

thirsty
dry
parched
thirst

Thinking about water can make you **thirsty**.

this

This is my pet armadillo, Sir Lancelot!

throw

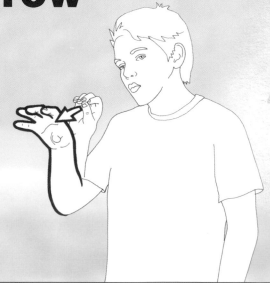

Throw the ball to the catcher!

thunder

Spot thinks **thunder** is too loud and scary!

Thursday

This year, my birthday is on **Thursday**.

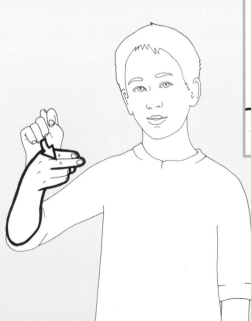

NOTE. **Thursday** can be signed two different ways.

a b c d e f g h i j k l m n o p q r s **t** u v w x y z

ticket

If you want to go to the theater, you need a **ticket**!

tie
knot

She stopped to **tie** her shoe.

tiger

The **tiger** is orange with black stripes.

time

He looked at his watch to see the **time**.

tired

fatigued

weary

After building walls all day, Little Pig is **tired**.

toast

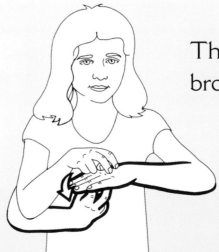

The **toast** is brown and crispy.

a
b
c
d
e
f
g
h
i
j
k
l
m
n
o
p
q
r
s
t
u
v
w
x
y
z

today

Yesterday we had social studies, and **today** we have science.

tomato

The farmer's **tomato** won the blue ribbon.

tomorrow

When he wakes up **tomorrow**, he will go fishing.

toothbrush

Always put toothpaste on your **toothbrush**.

toothpaste

WHITE & BRIGHT

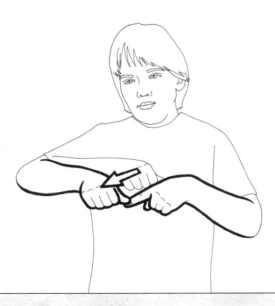

Toothpaste usually comes in a tube.

tornado

The **tornado** whipped across the farmland.

a b c d e f g h i j k l m n o p q r s t u v w x y z

total
sum

Altogether, she has a **total** of two kittens.

touch

The devil said, "Ignore the 'do not **touch**' sign."

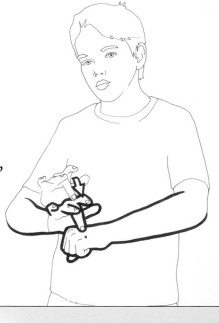

towel

How much hair is drying under that **towel**?

town
community
village

The seaside **town** was tranquil that fall afternoon.

train
railroad

The new **train** is going around the Christmas tree.

transportation

Many people use public **transportation** to travel around town.

a b c d e f g h i j k l m n o p q r s **t** u v w x y z

travel
tour

He rides a camel to **travel** across the desert.

tree

My dad put a tire swing on our **tree**.

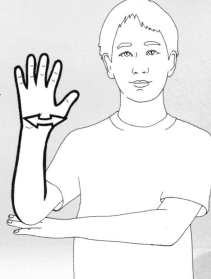

trip

Our family took a **trip** to Italy.

trophy
award
prize

The M.V.P. **trophy** was huge!

true
actual   really
am   sure
authentic   that's true
certain   truly
original
real

The **true** answer is the right answer.

try
make an effort

If at first you don't succeed, **try**, try again!

a
b
c
d
e
f
g
h
i
j
k
l
m
n
o
p
q
r
s
t
u
v
w
x
y
z

Tuesday

I have volleyball practice on **Tuesday**.

tunnel

The train went slowly through the **tunnel**.

turkey
Thanksgiving

The **turkey** has beautiful red tail feathers.

turn around

Turn around three times and pin the tail on the donkey.

turtle
tortoise

The **turtle** loves to swim!

TV
television

He made a **TV** costume.

a b c d e f g h i j k l m n o p q r s **t** u v w x y z

twins

a b c d e f g h i j k l m n o p q r s **t** u v w x y z

The brother and sister **twins** were born the same day.

type

She can **type** very fast on the computer.

Now, You Know

We have already mentioned how the meaning of a sign can change with its location (for example, *mother/father*). The location can also add information to the sign. When a signer describes pain, he shows the exact area that hurts. Making the sign for *pain* at the following locations creates a specific meaning:

Location	Meaning
forehead	I have a headache.
ear	I have an earache.
stomach	My stomach hurts.
back	My back hurts.
knee	My knee hurts.

Uu

ugly

The **ugly** troll will scare the goats with his horrible appearance.

umbrella

Shane stayed dry under the giant **umbrella**.

a b c d e f g h i j k l m n o p q r s t **u** v w x y z

uncle

Her mom's brother, **Uncle** Sam, is a sailor.

under
beneath

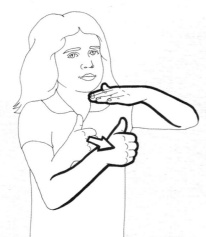

Pascal waits **under** the mistletoe for a kiss.

understand
comprehend
see

Spot can **understand** that his friend is sad.

United States

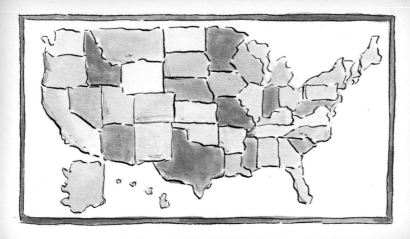

The **United States** of America became a country in 1776.

until

to

Baxter must wait **until** Christmas to open his gifts.

up

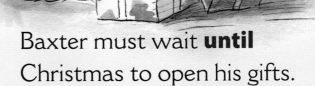

The rockets pushed him **up** high in the air.

NOTE. **Up** can be signed straight or at an angle, depending on the sentence.

a b c d e f g h i j k l m n o p q r s t u v w x y z

use
usage
useful
utilize

Miners **use** a pan to find gold in a stream.

Vv

vacation
holiday
leave

Chris is taking a trip during summer **vacation**.

variety

diverse
variation
varied
various

A one-man band plays a **variety** of musical instruments.

vegetables

Don't forget to eat your **vegetables**!

very

She was **very** upset when she lost the game.

visit

In the summer, he will **visit** his cousin's farm.

vitamin

Oranges are a good source of **vitamin** C.

vocabulary

She used a thesaurus to increase her **vocabulary**.

voice

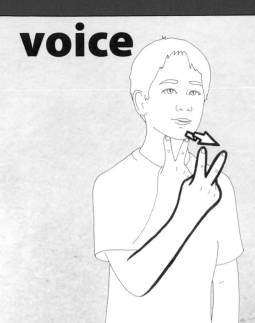

Attention everyone! I'm talking with my outside **voice**!

volleyball

Each **volleyball** team has six players.

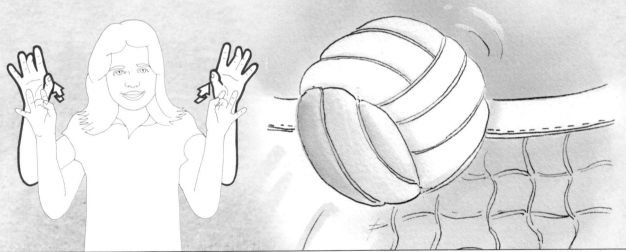

vote
elect

When you are 18, you can **vote** in elections.

a b c d e f g h i j k l m n o p q r s t u v w x y z

wait

He had to **wait** fifteen minutes for the bus to arrive.

walk

Andy likes to **walk** on his hands.

walk to

He grew big enough to **walk to** Mom.

wall

This **wall** is made of bricks.

want

Today, I **want** milk on my cereal.

war
battle

The army used tanks to fight in World **War** I.

wash

Use a soapy sponge to **wash** the dishes.

Washington, DC

Washington, DC is the capital of the United States.

watch

Birds can tell when you **watch** them.

water

Flowers need **water** and sunlight to grow.

water fountain
drinking fountain

Spot got a drink from the **water fountain**.

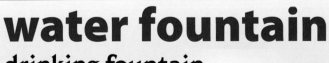

1

2

a
b
c
d
e
f
g
h
i
j
k
l
m
n
o
p
q
r
s
t
u
v
w
x
y
z

watermelon
melon

Watermelon tastes great on a hot summer day.

we
us

We both rode on the swan.

weather
climate

The **weather** man says it will rain today.

Wednesday

I have an appointment mid-week, on **Wednesday**.

week

I am going to camp for seven days, a full **week**.

weekend

Who doesn't love their **weekend** days off?

a b c d e f g h i j k l m n o p q r s t u v **w** x y z

weigh
pound
weight

How may pounds do I **weigh** this week?

west
western

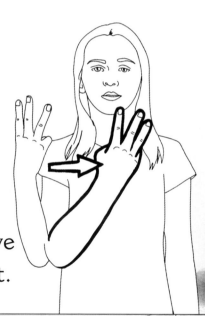

If we face **west**, we will see the sun set.

wet
damp
humid
moist
moisture

Some dogs love getting **wet**, but others don't.

whale

The blue **whale** is the largest animal in the world.

what

Waldo can't see **what** Spot is wearing.

whatever

anyhow
anyway
doesn't matter
even though
in spite of
nevertheless
no matter
regardless

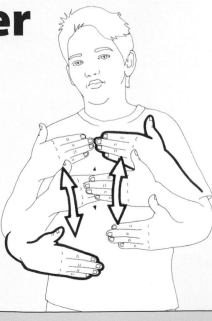

You can choose **whatever** dessert you want.

a b c d e f g h i j k l m n o p q r s t u v **w** x y z

wheels

A bicycle has two **wheels**.

wheelchair

When you are hurt and can't walk, use a **wheelchair**.

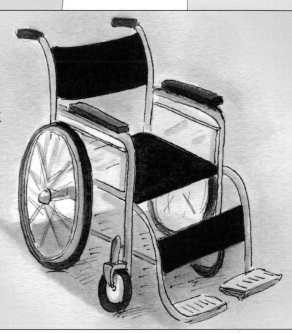

when

When will it be time for your cast to come off?

where

Where in the world have you been?

which

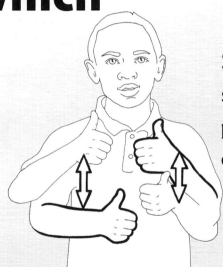

So many shoes—**which** pair should I choose?

white

White is an odd color for a snail.

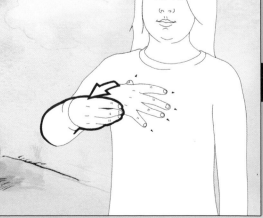

who

Guess **who** is behind you!

why

Tell me, **why** do I have to go?

wife

He carried his **wife** into their new house.

win

If the pictures are all the same, you **win** a prize!

wind
breeze
windy

The **wind** blew his papers across the room.

window

You can see through a **window**, not through a door.

a
b
c
d
e
f
g
h
i
j
k
l
m
n
o
p
q
r
s
t
u
v
w
x
y
z

witch

This **witch** is flying home on her broomstick.

with

Picking apples **with** you is more fun than doing it alone.

wolf

Instead of grandmother, she discovered the **wolf**!

woman

female
lady

Our police
chief is a
woman.

wonderful

excellent
fantastic
great
marvelous
outstanding
terrific

Her **wonderful** lamb
won the blue ribbon.

wood

Use the **wood**
to build a
doghouse.

a
b
c
d
e
f
g
h
i
j
k
l
m
n
o
p
q
r
s
t
u
v
w
x
y
z

word
vocabulary

We like to play **word** games with letters.

work
job
labor
task

Mickey helps his mom do **work** around the house.

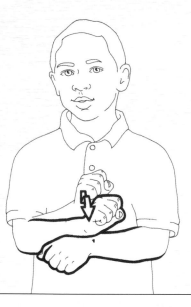

world

This **world** is round and full of living creatures.

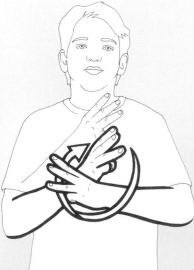

worm

The **worm** likes the hook better than the fish.

worry

anxious

fret

He won't **worry** unless he can't find his lost cat.

WOW

He said, "**Wow**! That is a giant peanut!"

a
b
c
d
e
f
g
h
i
j
k
l
m
n
o
p
q
r
s
t
u
v
w
x
y
z

write
handwrite

A long time ago, people would **write** with quills.

wrong

Four test answers are right and one is **wrong**.

TEST

-1

1. 1+1 = 2
2. 2+2 = 5 ✓
3. 3+4 = 7
4. 6+2 = 8
5. 3+1 = 4

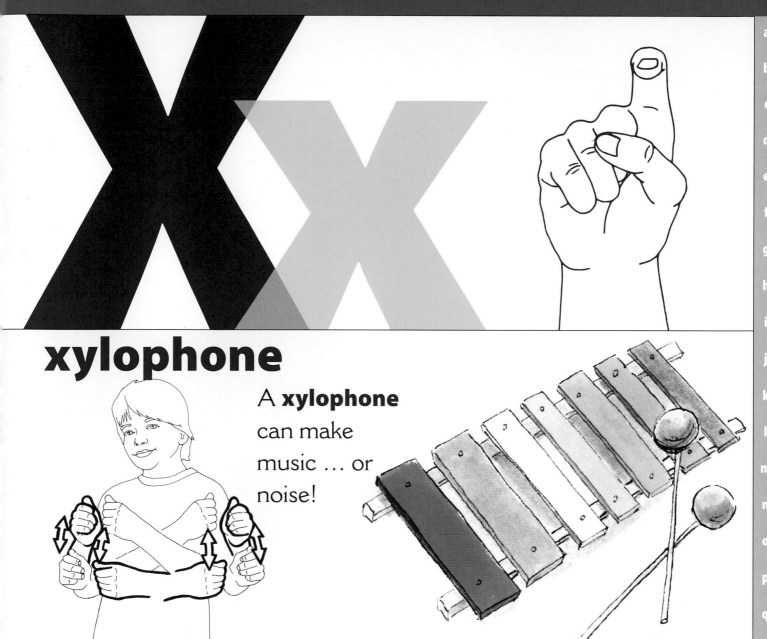

xylophone

A **xylophone** can make music … or noise!

Now, You Know

Languages create new words by combining two existing words into one word (a compound) with its own meaning. Some compounds in English include *somebody, playground,* and *nightgown.* ASL also has compounds, and some of these are

mother + father = parents
girl + marry = wife
boy + baby = son
think + same = agree
boy + same = brother
girl + same = sister

a
b
c
d
e
f
g
h
i
j
k
l
m
n
o
p
q
r
s
t
u
v
w
x
y
z

a b c d e f g h i j k l m n o p q r s t u v w x y z

Yy

year

The Titanic sank in the **year** 1912.

yellow

Brice is the captain of the **yellow** team.

yes

If you agree, mark "**yes**."

yesterday

Today is Tuesday, so **yesterday** was Monday.

you (singular)

You can do it, Mom!

a
b
c
d
e
f
g
h
i
j
k
l
m
n
o
p
q
r
s
t
u
v
w
x
y
z

you (plural)
you all

You all are doing a great job!

young
youngster
youth
youthful

Finn is 3 and that is too **young** to go to school.

your
yours

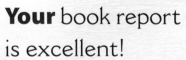

Your book report is excellent!

NOTE. To sign **yours**, move your hand from left to right.

yourself

You can do it! Pedal to make **yourself** go!

Zz

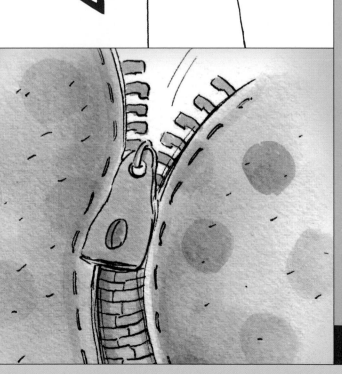

zipper

Pull up the coat **zipper** to stay warm.

a
b
c
d
e
f
g
h
i
j
k
l
m
n
o
p
q
r
s
t
u
v
w
x
y
z